I Remember
Tucking Mill

A memoir of his early life by

Stanley Wicks

was born at number five Tucking Mill Cottages, 8 October 1910.
other was Lavinia Owen, daughter of Isaac Owen, who then lived
anal Cottage, Monkton Combe. My father was William Wicks, son
William Wicks, of Vine Cottage, Monkton Combe.

My first memory of my childhood days was a fierce-looking rooster t
resided over a small group of Rhode Island Reds in a pen owned by
eighbour Mrs Bolton. She took me by the hand to the doorway of the
nd encouraged me to go in and collect a large brown egg that was just vis
n the nesting box. His majesty the cockerel barred my way and I was terrif
owever with a bit   ing pecked to de
nd collected the   k and she wat
ver us in a diplo   rose.

When a new   strange lady w
ome over the hill   Nellie. She w
it strict and kept   d pudding or b
rab apples were t   were told to pu
ur workaday rags   ol, presided ov
he Reverend War   ontrol again,
Nellie departed an   rough the field
he Bluebell Steps. On the way we collected wayside blossoms and stuffed
n her bag together with a few stinging nettles to liven her up.

Tucking Mill was indeed a fairyland to be born into. The brook bu
ontentedly past the bottom of the garden. Here it was joined by a stream
ushed from under the canal bank and wound its way through a ragged li
rees and bushes entangled with barbed wire. This formed a boundary be
he meadow and the cottage gardens. The Great Western Railway, c
een from our front door, provided us with the spectacle of steam engines dr
oal trucks to and fro at regular intervals. Now and again a motor

I Remember Tucking Mill

First published in Great Britain 2007 by
The Combe Down Heritage Society

Supported by Bath and North East Somerset
Council, Hydrock, Wessex Water and
Awards for All Lottery Fund 2007

Edited by Rosemary Simmons

Copyright © 2007 Combe Down Heritage Society

Designed by Lisa Pentreath

Printed by Emtone Printing Services Limited

ISBN 0-9550655-2-6

I Remember Tucking Mill

A memoir of his early life by Stanley Wicks

With seven short walks for today
as described by the author in the early 1920s

~

With prefaces by his two nieces
and his longest employer

~

Edited by Rosemary Simmons
Designed by Lisa Pentreath

Contents

Introduction

The manuscript of Stanley Wicks's memoir was offered to the Combe Down Heritage Society in 2006 by his surviving nieces and nephews who had such fond memories of their uncle.

The Society felt that this was an important document of life in a rural backwater just south of Bath, where the internal combustion engine was only just beginning to bring changes. At the time described, the Somersetshire Coal Canal had been closed since 1898 and was gradually silting up and being filled in places. The Somerset and Dorset Railway (the Slow and Dirty) was still running from the North through Bath and down to Bournemouth, going through a mile-long tunnel under Combe Down - Stanley Wicks describes it entering the tunnel near Tucking Mill on its way north again 'with an earthquake rumble'.

The Great Western Railway bought up old canal land and opened the Limpley Stoke to Camerton branch in 1910, the year Stanley Wicks was born; the line closed in 1951. The Fullers Earth Works closed in stages, and by 1945 it had gone from Tucking Mill. The land was bought by Wessex Water in the 1970s. Tucking Mill canal bridge is now half buried in a garden and can only be glimpsed through the fence. The mill itself was demolished in the 1927 but Tucking Mill Cottage with 'the fancy windows', once part of the mill, remains and erroneously bears a plaque to say that it was William Smith's house. His real house, Tucking Mill House, still stands just a little eastwards.

Stanley describes various rambles that he and his boyhood friends took from Tucking Mill. These have be separated out of the main text so that readers may easily walk in his footsteps and see what remains from the early twentieth century.

There have been some beneficial changes since Stanley Wicks lamented the ugliness of the Fullers Earth Works. Wessex Water have enlarged the lake and it now offers facilities to disabled fishers; The Avon Wildlife Trust have a nature reserve just off the path from Tucking Mill Lane to the Viaduct where considerate visitors are welcome; the most recent addition under the Right to Roam Act is to open an area between Shepherd's Walk and Midford Road.

Many people feature in the memoir, I have kept Stan Wicks's spelling of their names. The Combe Down Heritage Society would welcome further information about them, changes to the landscape as well as other memories of the area. Please contact me at 12 Greendown Place, Combe Down, Bath BA2 5DD.

Rosemary Simmons
Chair of Combe Down Heritage Society, 2007

Preface

What can I say about our Uncle Stanley except he was an extraordinary man. He was very intelligent (although some may say eccentric): he was very humourous, caring and thoughtful; he loved to chat about all manner of subjects (except domestic issues) - he would always say 'Auntie Gwen will fill you in on the domestics'.

We all loved spending time with him, whether it was in his cottage (No 1 Mount Pleasant) which he shared with his sister Gwendoline, in their very pretty garden, walking in the lanes, or sitting in his workshop (his 'den') discussing everything from, perhaps, a may bug that had hibernated in the corner of the room to the cumulus clouds that were gathering in the valley. He was full of stories of the past that were enthralling. One day we may have dressed up acting out a play he had written, complete with sound effects, which he filmed in one of the disused quarries around Mount Pleasant. The next day he would take us on a walk to the viaduct at Limpley Stoke teaching us about wild flowers along the way and telling us about our ancestors who lived in the lock keeper's cottage on the canal.

He would take us to the 'big house' (Monkswold) where he worked as a gardener, where one day, perhaps, he had built a stone wall and another had made a deterrent in the disguise of an animal to prevent foxes.

One of his many talents was poetry. Sometimes he would narrate them in front of a tape recorder and we would put in the sound effects: once I had to go and pull the toilet chain and another time throw some potatoes into an enamel bowl!

My thoughts of Uncle Stanley will always be of a very kind and patient man who was certainly unique in every way - it was a privilege having him as an uncle.

Carlene Fuller

A Tribute to Stanley Wicks

No. One Mount Pleasant was where I was born right there in Aunt Gwen's bedroom in December 1942. My parents Violet and Edward Brewer where married in December 1941 and Father, Stanley and Phillip Wicks were all in the Forces during World War II. My first memories of No. One was of Granny and Gramfer Wicks who were lovely grandparents. When my father was demobbed we left Mount Pleasant because it was bulging at the seams and moved to Bristol.

Later when I used to visit them it was just like going back in time - the old grey gas cooker was still there in the kitchen and a coal fire aglow in the living room with the old black kettle steaming on its trivet. In later years his one concession to modernisation was to have the lovely old gas lights replaced by electricity.

Whilst Stanley was in the army he became immensely interested in the wireless and radar - something he was unable to pursue as a career due to family circumstances. Stanley's father William was gardener to the big house, the occupants also owned the cottage in which the family lived. William had to retire so Stanley felt that his only option was to take over from his father to keep a roof over the family's head.

As you would expect, he became an expert at gardening and transformed the gardens of Monkswold into a kaleidoscope of colour.

Stanley's home was a children's paradise, even girls were allowed to take radios apart in his workshop. Our favourite uncle was a clever man; he taught himself to repair radios and then later televisions, so naturally, he ended up doing repairs for most of the neighbourhood and usually for nothing. If he had been born into this era he would most certainly have gone to university.

The endless comings and goings of children, friends and any waifs and strays who had an interesting tale to tell must have driven his sister Gwen mad, but she soldiered on making endless cups of tea and corned beef sandwiches. She looked after Stan because it was her sisterly duty to do so. Stan put no value on material things. If an old antique chair had a wonky leg a six-inch nail would solve the problem but if a sick plant could be saved he would look after it as if it was a baby.

In his declining years, Stanley still wrote stories taking his bag of pencils, paper and corned beef sandwiches to bed with him. Although his body became very frail his mind was as bright as that of the young lad who used to wander the fields and footways of Tucking Mill.

Pauline Upward

In Memory of Stanley Wicks

Stanley Wicks died in Osbourne House, Combe Down, on 16 September 1996. He had his lunch, returned to bed and quietly closed his eyes - an elegant way to go. But then, in his own way, Stanley was an elegant man. He had an elegance that was not in any way dependent on wealth, for he never had much wealth, and seemed to have little interest in the material world.

Except for five years service to his country, including participating in Dunkirk and the D-Day Invasion, experiences that made him a life-long pacifist, he spent his entire working life in the gardens of homes in the vicinity of Monkton Combe at wages that precluded any elegant luxuries.

Stanley's elegance was in what I would call the luxuriousness of his spirit. He was wholly involved with things that matter - how he should live in a natural world that held him in glorious awe, and how he should conduct himself in his relationships with his fellow men. Blessed with a fine, imaginative and inquiring mind, his elegant world was largely of his own creation. He never ventured further from the cottage he and his adored sister Gwendoline shared, than the bottom of his garden. I should say gardens, for Monkswold, where my wife and I live next door to Stanley, was his creation in the 35 years he worked there.

He did not seek to control the garden - he disliked pruning, pollarding and perfect patterns. He believed in Nature's abundance and saw himself as a steward. His love of the garden extended to its insects and animal residents and his way of coping with these predators, reflecting his generous spirit, was to plant enough for all.

We have all benefited from either his electronic skills or the delightful packets of seeds he made by the dozen; seeds gathered from the garden and packaged by hand in illustrated envelopes; or a spare part from his hoard of saved bits and pieces or just a thought expressed in the unique way in which he used language. These notes came through Monkswold's door - beside advice on every conceivable aspect of gardening, carried essays on subjects as diverse as Using greens in painting pictures, History of the Valley of Cume, In defence of the corned beef sandwich and A small history of pocket knives.

If ever there was a man of whom it could be said that he lived on in the hearts and minds of those whose lives he touched, that would be Stanley Wicks.

Walter McNeil
A Tribute to Stanley Wicks at his funeral

Stanley's mother Lavinia Wicks holding Gwen

Tucking Mill canal and cottages

Family Life

I was born at number five Tucking Mill Cottages, 8 October 1910. My mother was Lavinia Owen, daughter of Isaac Owen, who then lived at Canal Cottage, Monkton Combe. My father was William Wicks, son of William Wicks, of Vine Cottage, Monkton Combe.

My first memory of my childhood days was a fierce-looking rooster that presided over a small group of Rhode Island Reds in a pen owned by our neighbour Mrs Bolton. She took me by the hand to the doorway of the pen and encouraged me to go in and collect a large brown egg that was just visible in the nesting box. His majesty the cockerel barred my way and I was terrified, however with a bit of coaxing from Mrs Bolton, I risked being pecked to death and collected the egg. Mrs Bolton lived with her son Jack and she watched over us in a diplomatic way, always ready to help if need arose.

When a new member was added to our growing family a strange lady would come over the hill to take care of us. We called her Aunt Nellie. She was a bit strict and kept all available food for mealtimes. No bread pudding or baked crab apples were to be eaten between meals. On Sundays we were told to put on our workaday rags and only changed into our best to attend Sunday School, presided over by the Reverend Warrington. When mother was able to take over control again, Aunt Nellie departed and we kids escorted her up the Paddock, through the fields, to the Bluebell Steps. On the way we collected wayside blossoms and stuffed them in her bag together with a few stinging nettles to liven her up.

Tucking Mill was indeed a fairyland to be born into. The brook burbled contentedly past the bottom of the garden. Here it was joined by a stream that gushed from under the canal bank and wound its way through a ragged line of trees and bushes entangled with barbed wire. This formed a boundary between the meadow and the cottage gardens. The Great Western Railway, clearly seen from our front door, provided us with the spectacle of steam engines drawing coal trucks to and fro at regular intervals. Now and again a motor train would hurry by with a few passengers.

Our other railway, The Somerset and Dorset, comes into view half way down Twinhoe Hill, passing over the Midford Viaduct into Midford Station. The medley of sounds created on a stormy night, with an express leaving the station and attacking the gradient was an orchestration of magic. Akin to Schubert's *Unfinished Symphony*. Between the flare of the lightening flash, the crashing thunder claps echoing through the valley, the squally wind rustling the treetops and howling round the house. The big drops of rain spattering the windows and rattling the galvanised roof of the Fullers Earth Works and the peacocks giving cry from Midford Castle. As a steam train starts with piping whistle and roars along the embankment in an ever increasing crescendo of sound. Quietens momentarily through a cutting, then burst forth again over Tucking Mill Viaduct, then with a wailing whistle plunges into the black forbidding Combe Down Tunnel with an earthquake rumble and gone, leaving the peacocks and the elements to finish the piece.

The residents of Tucking Mill during the 1914 war were the Wicks family - at No. five: Gwendoline, Stanley, Phillip, Violet and Olive - at No. four were Mrs Bolton and Jack, her son - at No. three Granny West - at No. two Mr and Mrs Chapel and at No. one were Mr and Mrs Gerrish and their family of flowers (Lily, Daisy, Lucy, Gladiola, Iris, Arthur and Raymond). At Tucking Mill House were Mr and Mrs Palmer with Bert, Alec, Pearl and Ruby. At Tucking Mill Cottage were Mr and Mrs Morris with Alec, George, Vera, William, Leslie and Bertha.

The first family to leave us was the Chapels. They were very old and when one dies the other was shuffled off to the workhouse. This was the stone building with the clock now part of St Martin's Hospital. Jack Harris, carpenter and decorator of Brewery Yard, Monkton Combe, was given the job by Mr Freeman of the Mill and also landlord of the cottages, to delouse and generally clean the place out. The bedding was dumped on the cabbage patch and burned. Jack gave an occasional scratch as the fleas jumped for their very lives.

The incoming tenants at No. two were Mr and Mrs Cross and Austin, Doris and Leonard; two daughters came later. Then Mrs Bolton died and her son left Tucking Mill. The new tenant was scruffy, middle-aged, amiable Tommy Dandridge. He worked in the garden at the College (Monkton Combe School. Ed.). I well remember Tommy on the sick list with a poisoned foot, after driving the point of a sickle into his ankle, owing to his dislike of soap and water it festered. Doctor Norris (this might be Morris. Ed.) arrived one day to administer to him and asked mother for some hot water to bathe the injured part. Mother applied the purifying liquid and Tommy let out a yell that startled the cows in the meadow. The good Doctor cried with some severity, 'Don't boil the man, woman'. Tommy did not stop with us very long but took up residence nearer his work as soon as it became available.

Father must have been feeling rich for the first time on his thirty bob a week for he took the drastic action of renting No. four as well. Mr Harris arrived to make a doorway in the back kitchen wall. Living conditions at this time were rudimentary. The water supply did come out of a tap, but it only came across the canal from the spring. It was similar to life in a caravan, water had to be carried in buckets and a slop pail was always available for tea leaves and washing up water and probably went on the garden. The toilet was a double-seated affair, and had a drain to the brook that needed plenty of water from the tap fifty yards away. The big houses were worse off, having a bucket under a seat in some dingy corner. The water had to be carried from the spring. There were no services, other than the telephone to Tucking Mill House. The illumination was by oil lamps and candles. The heating and cooking was done by coal fire. I thought it was rather like a couch fire on the allotment: the fire was kindled with the aid of dry twigs, a good base was put in with coal and cinders, with peelings, tea leaves, and just anything that would burn topped off with small coal. This mixture would guarantee a good fire for four hours at least. Of course there was a lot of ash to clear out next day, but that was no problem there was plenty of room on the garden for it.

I well remember the rosy glow created by the fire and a shaded oil lamp on a winter's night and the guttering candles we carried as we set off for bed. There was a massive kitchen table in the centre of the living room, used for all purposes. It was the rule of the times to scrub everything with hot water, soap and soda. The women wore aprons and wielded the scrubbing brushes as they knelt on kneeling pads and cleaned a patch at a time.

My parents were educated on a two pence a week basis in a small school at the top of Mill Lane, Monkton Combe. The education was elementary and enabled them to read and write and to count the few shillings of survival. Mother endeavoured to clothe us by making use of any material available. With her hand-cranking sewing machine she would stitch together bits she had salvaged from adult garments to make up something fit for us kids. Patching and darning was the order of the day and even when the garment was finally discarded, it made useful house flannel. Squares of hessian from old sacks made useful towels for wiping the hands and also mats on which to wipe our muddy boots.

She also needed to be a magician in relationship to food. The status symbol in those days was a big iron pot. Into this went cheap cuts of meat, whole rabbits cut up, bones of many sorts and every kind of vegetable. With a suitable quantity of liquid, it would simmer away and provide food for the whole family.

I well remember early one Friday evening, mother put on her hat and coat for her weekly journey to the Co-Op to collect the weekly goods. She had no money and knew she would get no goods unless she settled for those delivered the previous week. At half past five mother took off her hat and coat and put on the big iron pot. Father must have been out of work at the time and was out looking for work that would allow him to bring home some money - that day he failed. If all else failed, the iron pot would provide something. Mother was a champion potato peeler. There always seemed to be small ones, these she would twirl with her left hand while applying the knife with the right. Usually the peel came off in one long piece. If potato peelings were not used to bank up the fire, they found their way to Mr Morris's pig and when the unlucky creature was turned into pork, we usually received a choice portion.

On Sundays mother made a cake and on our return from Sunday School the smell of burnt currants always assailed our nostrils. The oven situated at the side of the fire-grate was luke warm one side and red hot the other. Consequently in the process of cooking it burned on one side and it was necessary to turn it round and burn the other side to make certain that it was cooked in the middle. I dislike burnt cake, but did not throw it away, but always ate the black part first in order to enjoy what was left. Mother's other cooking accomplishments were plenty of bread pudding and a kind of toffee made of brown sugar. Father also had a bent for cooking, his speciality was bloaters. These he would place on top of the fire. He would sit surveying the whole house with a dreadful stink. When he thought the fish was sufficiently done one side he would turn it over with the toasting fork and burn the other side. After a suitable time the black mass was manoeuvred on to a plate and tea was ready. He also had a great liking for bubble and squeak. Plenty of mashed potato was piled into a frying pan and a quantity of greens added, with the addition of a little dripping or even lard and plenty of pepper and salt. The mass was mixed together over a suitable fire and the result was a cheap and appetising meal for all who wished to partake. If the greens were in short supply, a few sliced onions were equally good.

Other favourites were milk sop, not heard much of nowadays. This was a piece of stale bread soaked in hot water with milk added and well sugared. Then there was the more economical one called kettle broth. Pieces of bread in hot water with pepper and salt. Toast was always a favourite, one might call it a cheap luxury. It always seemed quite difficult to get enough glowing coals in the same place to hold your bread to and get that lovely golden brown. Of course if beef dripping or butter was available it was indeed a luxury, I cannot remember much fresh butter - margarine and lard seemed to feature in most meals. Father was very good at trapping rabbits and admitted to have been a bit of a poacher in his time.

He was good at using a scythe, this implement was a bent stick with offset handles. The blade was fixed by a tang in a ring at the bottom end by a small iron wedge. Every blade had to be hung by a blacksmith at an angle to suit the operator so that he was under the minimum of strain when mowing. It was a sight worth seeing when a number of men kitted out with whetstones in leather carriers attached to their belts set out to mow a field. Each one a convenient distance behind the other would swing their blades in unison and cut swathes after swathes until the job was done - a veritable work of art.

Father also had a double barrelled gun, its purpose was to destroy vermin. One day a whole family of rats emerged from behind the hen house and father destroyed the lot with one blast. Although he boasted of taking large eels and jacks from the canal, his fishing activities were confined to dropping a baited hook on the end of a line supported on a nut stick in the brook at the bottom of the garden and visiting it at meal times.

He also told us stories of the cold days of the past when the canal was frozen over and we would rent a stretch and armed with a brush, keep the ice clear of fragments, whilst charging skaters a penny to use his section. He said that the unscrupulous ones would half sever the straps as they fixed the skates of some of their customers and when the strap snapped they would produce another from their pockets to replace it, for a few pence, of course. It was noticeable in the early part of the century that winters were colder and the summers hotter than they are today. The fields near the brook, owned by farmer Fletcher and mill owner Oburn were set up to allow them to be flooded and used as skating rinks, earning a nice bit of currency as the sporting public came to frolic on the ice.

There were no radios or televisions in those days and people made their own entertainment. Father was musical and had a melodeon, which he endeavoured to play. There was also a cylinder gramophone. The cylinder was placed over a drum which revolved under the influence of a spring and a needle attached to a sound box picked up the tune. The quality was so bad that it was a relief to get to the end of the recording. Whenever we visited Aunt Francis, who lived next door to my Grandfather Owen at Monkton Combe, we were usually regaled with Layton Johnston singing *River stay away from my door*, especially when the floods were up, of course.

Stanley in a school photo, 1918 (he is in the middle row, with the sailor hat)

Childhood Pursuits

The girls of Tucking Mill were always swinging their skipping ropes and marking squares in the road to play hopscotch. The boys were more inclined to be destructive and tried out bows and arrows, but then found catapults more satisfying in smashing bottles. There was always a great search going on through the woods and hedges to find a stick in the shape of a Y. Nature always seemed to be bit lopsided and did not provide a true catapult stick readily. Elastic was another problem, Bill and Arthur Gerrish managed to get real square catapult elastic from the shop. The rest of us were lucky if we got some strips of motor inner tube from the tip.

The pea shooter was quite popular with the smaller boys. This was eight inches of elder stick with the pith removed, and with a piece cut out of the side, giving a long barrel at front and a short one at the rear. A piece of steel bent rather like a question mark was inserted in the channel revealed and by pulling the front member back and using the loop as a trigger, peas or match sticks could be propelled into somebody's ear.

Another simple weapon was the sling, not the one David used on Goliath, this was a piece of ash stick with a slit cut at one end. By jamming a pebble in the slit and making a throwing action, not letting go of the stick, the pebble would be projected at least twice as far than in the ordinary way.

I also remember the bomb: this was a commercial affair in two metal sections which were looped together with a piece of string - caps were available in small half-penny boxes. One would be inserted between the two bomb sections and holding it on the string you dropped it behind some unsuspecting person, resulting in a nice bang and, perhaps, a clip around the ear hole.

The dangerous one was the hollow key with a nail pushed down the barrel; the two were joined with a long string. The key was loaded with a few red match heads and, with the nail in contact with them, was made to strike a convenient wall causing a small explosion. This form of entertainment is not to be encouraged as it has been known for the key to disintegrate.

During the cold months of the year, winter warmers were all the rage. A piece of rag was made to smoulder inside a perforated tin complete with a lid, and attached to a wire or string. You then whirled it around and around your head, endangering the lives of you companions, creating a nice draught through the holes in the tin thus speeding up the conflagration within. This gave warmth to the operator but severely polluted the atmosphere.

Like most boys, we had a great desire to obtain wheels of any description to put on trucks or guiding trolleys. I did manage to get one trolley made. The front wheels were fitted to a section of timber that was fitted to the main structure with one single nut and bolt. This allowed the contraption to be steered by means of a piece of rope, the ends attached the the woodwork near each front wheel. When my elder sister started work at fourteen in the Junior School, Combe Down, my brother and I used to accompany her back up the hill at night on her half-day off. The real reason for going was not so much to please my sister, but to race down Shaft Road at speed with the candle lantern showing the way and usually finishing in the ditch.

The Morrises had bicycles and the rest of us were very envious. We were always on the look out for bicycle parts, we never expected to find one complete. Then one day I found a frame on the rubbish heap complete with one wheel - the front one. There were no tyres, pedals or saddle but nearby another set of handlebars. Where could we get another wheel?. Short of paying money for it there was none to be had. Suddenly I had an inspiration, we did have an old wheelbarrow wheel. How could it be fitted in the rear forks? We gave it a try, securing it with thick wire; the spare handlebars were set in the saddle pillar for a saddle and we took it in turns to clatter down Tucking Mill Hill. It was a rough ride with the back wheel slapping against the forks.

Then George Morris presented us with a back wheel he had had to discard, owing to the fact that the brake blocks had worn a hole in the rim. I decided that it was not properly worn out yet and quickly removed the wheelbarrow wheel and fitted the back wheel. For a few days our bike went like a charm - the smoothness and speed was out of our world, then without much rim to hold the spokes, the back wheel folded up. Back we went to our trusty wheelbarrow wheel.

Then calamity struck: young Leslie Morris wanted a ride and when cornering at speed around the corner approaching the Fullers Earth Works, allowed his knee to contact the road and received severe lacerations to it. When my Father was told of the event, he flew into a rage and took it out on the bike, and left it twisted on the ash heap. For a whole week I implored Father to let me have my bike back. At last he gave way and we set out to straighten the front wheel that had received most of the big boot. No amount of effort would make that wheel revolve inside the forks without touching so we discarded that bike, our first one, with great sorrow.

The level stretch of road by the old mill was used extensively as a playground. On the old canal wharf nearby there was always a heap of flint stones to repair the road. Grandfather Owen, in his declining years, had the job of cracking them in to suitable sizes for his work. I well remember grandfather saying to me, after I had returned from a ramble to Midford. 'I was going to give you a three-penny piece to get down in the cut to lift one or two wayward stones, but seeing you wasn't here, I done it myself, anyway you can still have the three-penny piece'. Such was the good nature of Grandfather Owen. He was about eighty at the time and quite a number of grandfather's flints were flung upon the galvanised roof of the Works and as they banged and clattered back down we were delighted at the noise they made, and ran away in great excitement as the workmen ran out to catch us. As we played hide and seek in the dusk of a summer evening, the bats from the mill flew overhead with peculiar little squeaks as they fed off the midges.

Tucking Mill Cottage was a place of ornate windows and a porch with honeysuckle. What seemed an unnecessary passageway between the house and Back Lane, took us to the back yard with, perhaps, a bicycle by the wall near the back door. Across the yard was the toilet and up a step to the stables where there was odour and a grunting pig. This smelly animal was always an attraction to small children. A door at the rear took you to the garden and the view of the ghastly mess of galvanised iron that was the Fullers Earth Works. Through the back door of the Cottage, I do remember a small narrow room which was part of the mill and, therefore, seemed to have some mystery about it. It was here that Vera introduced me to barley meal cake. I think it was a 'copy mother making cake' experiment. I suppose mother said 'you are not wasting my flour, it costs money' so Vera had to resort to the pig's barley meal sack, mixed up with water, with addition of some sugar. She got permission to bake it in the oven and, what is more, it was palatable, although, I don't think Vera would have got any volunteers to eat her concoction if it had not been for the sugar.

Crossing the viaduct there used to be a group of towering beeches on the slope. We kids spent a lot of time there swinging on the branches - it was most exciting and rather dangerous. You grabbed a branch and walked backwards dragging it with you to its fullest extent, then you let it go forward and went with it hanging on for dear life. In this way you could swing out eight feet from the ground from the sloping ground; if your hand slipped or the branch broke you went down with an awful bump.

Then I remember the awful day when some workmen arrived with some winching gear, crosscut saws and axes; we watched with great excitement as the end of the hawser was attached high up in the tree. A notch was made in the falling side, then the crosscut went to work, a wedge was driven in behind the saw, the two men gave the crosscut a few more strokes then everyone stood back as the steam engine down in Back Lane tightened the hawser and the forest giant gave a groan and started to fall. The branches crumpled under the weight of the trunk and the ground shook under the impact as the tree hit the bank like a small cyclone. The rest of the group were accounted for in the same way and the vandals departed leaving a sad sight of nature distorted.

I remember we also climbed on a splendid cordon of lime trees; they were very difficult owing to the twiggy bits at the base. We looked for the scutty wrens nests that were always there, and we had a special branch that hung over the track that lead to Castle Woods; the branch was about seven feet from the ground and we used it as an endurance test. Each contestant was required to swing up and grab it with both hands and see how long he could hang on while we counted. Nobody ever seemed to win this contest, but there were plenty of competitors.

The slopes of the Park were made use of when it snowed; here on the gentle inclines we could try out our home made sledges. I also remember searching the hollow railway fence posts for blue tits nests. Although the Park was grazed by the occasional group of horses or cows, the soil was very poor and had its own special plants; there were harebells, catsear and sometimes a bee orchid. At the bottom of the Park were some more delectable beech trees glowing in the autumn sun in yellow, red and gold. Above the bank that drops away toward the canal, is a mysterious depression scooped out in the grass and usually full of leaves - we played in there never knowing what it was intended for. Below the bank by the wall and the built-in gateway near Tucking Mill Cottage, was an accumulation of leaf mould that nobody seemed to make use of.

I remember the giant shire horses owned by Mr Heal, timber haulier of Combe Down. Mr Mattock, who now lived in one of the cottages, worked for Mr Heal, and was required on Saturday to take the horses to pasture in Castle Park. We kids used to waylay him along Tucking Mill Lane and beg for a ride. Mr Mattock never refused our plea and helped us up on the broad backs. After a few such excursions, he would leave us at the bridge and we took the horses on to the Park, put water from the stream into their trough and shut them in for the weekend. Of course the horses knew where they wanted to go and needed very little directive from us.

Although the Morrises found a football to kick about, very often a leather case with a pig's bladder in, we never played the game very seriously. There were never any goal posts, just a couple of heaps of garments at either end of what was supposed to be the pitch.

The one consuming occupation was bathing in the brook. Near to the fallen poplar there was, if you like to call it that, the Tucking Mill bathing complex. First of all there is the 'ones' where the water is shallow, running over the stones and beneath the trees. Here the paddlers make themselves cold, wet and uncomfortable, but it gives them much enjoyment to rush back up the muddy bank to bask in the meadow sunshine. A little further along towards Midford, the water deepens and there is a convenient branch sticking out of the bank to take your weight while you splash furiously to get your circulation going as this is a cold and shaded place. This is called the 'fives'. Here you are supposed to learn to swim with the aid of water wings. The ones we used were two large stoppered tins tied together with string on which we were supported. The swimmers went a little father round to the 'fourteens'. This was a wide bay in the bend of the stream and, despite a fallen tree at the side of it, the water was very deep. Here the sun shone warmly on a good day and the best swimmers ran from the meadow and dived in from the high bank. Mr Humphris from Combe Down, a sailor, would climb the alder tree and dive from there. I remember the day I discarded my treacle tins and struck out across the 'fourteens' unsupported. I was amazed I did not sink to the bottom - it was so easy to swim.

A little farther on where the brook begins to narrow, was a more select bathing place - we called it Sandy Bottom. The deep water was on the meadow side, so it was better to go to the railway side, if you were prepared to scrabble over the fallen poplar. You then had to follow the stream along a tortuous path where sometimes the brook and the railway embankment came together and you were in danger of sliding into the water, and at other times a bit of pasture appeared and there was adequate room. I well remember a hilarious incident that occurred here: Reggie, who came from Mount Pleasant, was cavorting among the daisies at the top of the bank near Sandy Bottom, when he decided to attack a dry post sticking out of the ground. The object of his attention was far more brittle than he had anticipated and it gave way far too quickly for Reggie, and he was precipitated downward through a bed of stinging nettles to the water's edge. Was Reggie's face red. I'll say it was, right down to his toes, after all he was wearing his birthday suit.

The brook meanders its way south-westward: now and again a water rat plops into the water from the bank and dives for his doorway under the water line. The moorhen gives cry as it flaps along the surface of the stream. Sometimes you may catch sight of a kingfisher perched on a log ready to pounce on an unsuspecting fish.

Sometimes there was noise and confusion in the valley as the huntsmen and hounds came to hunt the otter - with very little result. The dogs spent most of the time chasing rabbits; I don't even remember seeing an otter.

Half way along the meadow was a bent willow, the trunk was split so you could walk through. Up inside it was dry and rotten, and a small fire I lit set the base of the tree on fire. It was curious to see a tree belching smoke like a steam engine. As usual I could not put it out so I made off trying to make out I wasn't there. Surprisingly, nobody seemed interested and the fire burnt itself out, and must have benefited the tree for it has only just been cut down.

The brook continues to wriggle its way toward Midford, getting father from the Great Western and closer to the Somerset and Dorset. As the drain from the canal culvert crosses our path, we leave the broad expanse of meadow land and a mere strip of pasture that lies between the brook and the towpath retaining wall. Soon we reach the spring and the watercress beds. The brook now deviates southward and dives under the Frome Road and divides, one arm going to Midford Mill and beyond and the other to Combe Hay.

Here in my teens in the depression of the thirties, I got a job hay making - I well remember being sent to the Old Post Office to recharge the ale jar. I was curious to taste the stuff, so I upended the jar going up Chapel Hill to sample the drop remaining. It was horrible and I tipped the rest in the road. On my return to the hayfield with a fresh supply, I was amazed as the grown ups tipped it down with evident relish and with great smacking of lips.

Near the hayfield, where the railway bridge crosses the Frome Road, there had been built a temporary halt for the convenience of anticipated passengers on the motor train. Very few took advantage of it as people said you couldn't go anywhere so why bother? We kids were faintly interested in this line but our favourite was the Somerset and Dorset. The trains made more noise and they went faster. Funny thing, nobody who lived at Tucking Mill seemed to ride on it - perhaps everybody was too poor. I know that around Christmas, if we kids went to Bath on the tram, it was only to see the decorations and to be able to look in the shop windows - we never thought of buying anything - it was other people who did that.

The Tram arriving from Bath at Rainbow Woods in 1938

Looking down from the viaduct at the Fullers Earth Works, Tucking Mill

Tucking Mill, attached to Tucking Mill cottage, far left

The Fullers Earth Works

The Fullers Earth Works sprawled in the valley in a misshapen mass of galvanised iron - inside it looked a bit more orderly.

Towards the top of Horsecombe Brook there was a large drum suspended on pillars round which was wound a wire rope, the ends of which were connected to a number of trucks in a train. One end to a set of trucks going down, and the other end to the front of empty ones coming up. There was also 'The Pan', a large mortar mixer. Part of Horsecombe Brook water was lead in to mingle with fullers earth that had been tipped in, and the rollers turned the mixture into a slurry which then departed down the pipeline. Some of the mineral was mined in the locality in the earlier years. Tunnels were driven into the hillside and propped up inside with pit props. The workings were treacherous and some of the workmen got buried as the roof caved in. Eventually, I think, the mineral came from the workings beyond the Burnt House at Odd Down, taking this unusual route.

Behind the stables of Tucking Mill Cottage were a number of settling tanks in a straight row, alongside these were openings leading to a number of iron-plated steam kilns. This side of the works covered territory at least a hundred yards long in a north-westerly direction. Beyond this, towards the railway, is a tall chimney to take away the smoke and fumes of the two furnaces. Nearby is another large settling tank and a nice crab apple tree, from which came our baked crab apples that we were so fond of.

Over on the north-eastern side was another settling tank much in use in the twenties - the fullers earth in suspension, was carried down the pipeline from Odd Down and diverted into the settling tank. The heavy sand sank immediately on entry to the bottom of the tank whilst the mineral in suspension floated to all parts before settling and a pure product was available. The water was gradually drained away through a sluice of removable boards in slots. A set of rails was laid between the tank and the steam kiln and a trolley trundled along it.

The workmen dressed in corduroys and clogs with spats of sacking, shovelled the wet mineral into the trolley and then unloaded it on to the steam kiln. When it was partially dry, it was transferred to the fire kiln to complete the process. The product, now walnut-sized, was shovelled on to a large iron plate which was located over the culvert carrying the Horsecombe Brook towards the Midford Brook. One evening the stoker, Arthur Gerrish, was standing on a heap of granules that he had just removed from the fire kiln, when the iron plate caved in and precipitated Arthur and a good part of the heap into the culvert. Arthur's cries for help brought Mr West on the scene, and Arthur was dragged from a watery grave.

In the early days a frequent visitor to this area was Granny West, collecting oddments for her fire, sometimes a lump of coal that had strayed from the heap near the road, found its way into her folded apron. If the foreman of the works remonstrated with her she would say it was only a piece of stone that might block up the furnace. We kids were very helpful, stuffing sticks into her apron and sometimes pieces of horse dung.

Near the fire kiln was a pair of weighing scales with hooks for holding the sacks as the mineral was shovelled in and two-hundredweight was recorded on the scales. The top of the sack was then sewn up with string with the aid of a large string needle. On the south-eastern end of the fire kiln was a wall supporting the roof, on the other side of which was the fire kiln furnace set in a sort of well. I remember the glowing clinkers being removed from the firebars to the floor to be doused with water, then to be taken by wheelbarrow to the ash heap. I remember the giant ash heap where the evening primroses grew in profusion, and displayed their yellow blossoms in the gathering dusk to attract moths with their peculiar scent.

Directly opposite the fire kiln was the steam boiler and furnace and between the two on the south-west side, was the steam engine for pumping water into the boiler. In front there was a large box cushioned with a sack for the comfort of the stoker, hung above this was an evil-smelling lamp with just a wick and without a globe - rather like the magic lamp of Alladin. It was a very draughty place to be in, one side completely open to the elements. Coal was loaded on a large metal shovel-shaped wheelbarrow and trundled down the slope from the road. The stoker's duty was to keep the fire burning fiercely, keeping the steam pressure up, removing the ashes and clinker when it was necessary and shovelling on the coal. Meanwhile, he was required to do other jobs about the works.

Periodically the steam boiler fire was allowed to go out in order to de-scale it. The furnace was constructed with one cylinder of steel fitted inside the other with a suitable front and back riveted on, with a pressure gauge and doors The fire went inside the centre cylinder and the water circulated between the inner and outer. On top of the outer was a manhole, complete with cover, washered and bolted, to preserve the steam pressure. With this cover removed, my father and myself used to climb inside and straddle the inner tube. With a candle stuck in a lump of wet fullers earth for illumination, we chipped away the scale adhering to the inner cylinder. The scale dropped to the bottom and was extracted through a hole in the face of the furnace. It was a most unpleasant job, not one to be recommended to sufferers of claustrophobia. For three days labour I received the princely sum of half-a-crown.

On the north-eastern side of the fire kiln was the men's dressing room. A very simple affair, just a plank seat where they sat to put on their clogs and a bit of sacking. A flurry of wire nails in the plank wall took care of the discarded clothing. On the south-eastern side of the dressing room was a loading bay; a trolley on rails conveniently level with the floor of the works, was loaded with two-hundredweight sacks by use of sack trucks. Then, after the order had been given to Messrs Hamlen, and they had arrived with a wagon and six horses, the loaded trolley was hauled up to the road by means of wire rope wound round a wheel at the top of the incline, powered by a small steam engine in a shed by the coal supply. Later, when Hamlen went over to lorries, the trolley way was replaced by a cement road enabling the haulage vehicle to go straight to the loading bay. The fee paid to Hamlen for transporting two tons of fullers earth to the railway siding was thirty shillings.

Next door to Tucking Mill Cottage was the Mill which was probably turning out the finished article during the last century. We, as kids, used to crawl about in there, gaining entrance by a flap-door near the road. Climbing up a ladder to the top floor, we were able to view a hopper with a chain of iron cups that, apparently, picked up the powdered fullers earth where it had been dropped by two huge grinding stones down below, and deposited in the hopper. It was then led into suitable containers to be let down through the trap doors over the road into a conveyance or it could have been loaded on a barge on the canal.

The Mill was a place of bats, cobwebs and grey powder. The whole of the works was a labyrinth of wooden joists and angle brackets. In the summer, a place of chattering swallows that returned every year to build their nests of mud in the roof timbers, flying incessantly to and fro to feed on the swarms of flies that inhabited the atmosphere of Tucking Mill.

The Horsecombe Brook ran under the works and was called the Trunkall. This separated the Parish of Monkton Combe from that of South Stoke, in the latter was Tucking Mill House. The fact that William Smith, Father of English Geology, could have lived there did not impress us much, but somehow gave the building an atmosphere of its own. Mr Morris the tenant in those far off days, worked for the Fullers Earth Company but most likely was employed at the Pan, rather than at the Tucking Mill works. I think they all got a turn at that small establishment sometime or other.

I remember Jackie Williams telling me how he saved father's life one lunch hour, near the Pan. It seems that father had taken his ferret with him to work and used part of the lunch hour to try and entice a rabbit to come out of its burrow. However, the ferret killed the rabbit underground and remained with it. Father valued that ferret, and so he endeavoured to go head first down what was rather a big burrow. He got stuck and could not get out. Luckily Jackie was there and took him by the legs and hauled him back out.

Boiler delivery at the Fullers Earth Works

Moving House

We all measure our lives by the milestones along it - I suppose one such milestone was the departure of the Palmers from Tucking Mill House. This must have been about 1920 or thereabouts and I had no inkling that it was going to happen. It was a case of here today and gone tomorrow. I was sorry to lose the company of Alec - he was the adventurous one, always up to something. It was exciting to leave the cottage and move to a mansion and to have the freedom of a large estate. It was saddening really to have all those apple trees so that it was therefore unnecessary to steal other people's fruit.

I remember a white paling gate that led in from the road, with a pine tree on the left near a quickset hedge that ran down to the Fullers Earth Works. On the right hand side was a hedge mainly of snowberry, concealing a small lawn and a little arbor with a laburnum and a few fir trees; There was a lean-to greenhouse in front of the house with a bit of garden and rose trees. There was a laurel hedge leading from the pine tree to a willow that bowed conveniently across the way to allow a rope to be flung over to make a swing. Here too is a door leading to the cellar, a dingy stone-floored place, with a sink and a pump, put in by Mr Palmer, and an old-fashioned wash boiler. It was a storage place for potatoes and the mice who came to eat them; there was a window that looked into the inside of the greenhouse. From the cellar were some massive stone steps that took you to a passageway that went through the house. At one end was the front door which could also be reached by more stone steps outside from the door of the cellar. Near to the front door was the door to the front room; nobody ever seemed to go in there - it was cold and a bit posh. More comfortable was the living room at the other end of the passage - here there was always a fire and a big kitchen table. More stone steps lead up to three bedrooms; also from the main passage were more stone steps leading to the back kitchen where the coal was stored in a heap in the corner.

Here I remember the drowning of a litter of kittens. Aunt Francis had arrived from Monkton Combe to perpetrate the foul deed. I was unaware of this until I heard the plaintive cries of the victims coming from the back kitchen and I went to investigate. Four kittens were struggling for their lives in a pig's bucket half filled with water, a square chopping block had been placed on the outside rim of the bucket to stop the condemned from escaping. I was so unhappy about the state of affairs that I put my boot into the side of the bucket and holed it allowing water to escape in a flood. It did not save the kittens, Auntie finished them off with the chopping block.

The drinking water had to be carried from the spring and the children were expected to do it - they did not take it too seriously, and most of the water was spilled in the roadway. During our first year at Tucking Mill House the bucket lavatory under the Paddock was discontinued and a flush one fitted in the corner of the back kitchen. The snag was, of course, that all the water used had to be pumped up from the cellar by a pipe into a big supply tank. However, we could proudly boast that Tucking Mill House was the first to have a telephone and a flush lavatory.

I remember a small shrub by the front door where an orange blossom grew and gave scent in early summer. There was a grindstone where father ground his beloved scythe as I laboriously cranked the handle. There was an old hen house left by the Palmers and a small tunnel under the Paddock by the old lavatory. There were large red apples by the fullers earth trolley way, also a weedy patch on the other side of the plot parallel to the road and near the ash heap. We did not use it enough to keep the weeds down, near the half way mark was a cesspool on one side and a well on the other - a good combination I thought!

Nearby were black currants and gooseberry bushes; they did quite well in the clay soil. Along the north side of the ash heap was a line of very tall worthless apple trees. The ground was so poor that potatoes father planted underneath struggled to survive and the yield of tubers was farcical. What I do remember about this plot was the tenacity of the weeds that I was required to drag from their moorings - it was a terrible chore. Above the barren plantation was a grass path leading along to an old pigsty; here was a Tom Putt apple tree (an old west country cider apple. Ed) leaning like a bent old man but the rosy striped fruit was nice. A little farther on was a codlin which bore a juicy yellow fruit with a rib down the side. Behind the pigsty was a damson tree and in the sty we kept ducks - there were good layers. Mother even had some to spare and sold them to the Co-Op. One day she fed the ducks with left-over slices of cocoa butter and the Co-Op manager refused to buy any more because he said the customers complained at the brown steaks in the eggs. When the pen door was opened in the morning the five ducks followed the one drake along to the watercress beds; sometimes they left an egg there. The last time I saw those ducks was when they were led by the drake over the bridge to the meadow and Midford Brook. They never came back.

30

Along past the watercress beds near the railway was a wild area uncultivated, uncared for and boggy, there was an exit to the back lane. On the outskirts of the wooded area was a very big Blenheim Orange apple tree. The apples were delicious, but few in number; nobody ever attempted to pick them but they were allowed to fall and we kids were usually around to discover them. Back along the bank towards the pigsty was a very tall cherry tree, although we investigated it, it never bore any fruit. Towards the end of our stay at Tucking Mill House, the grassland was allowed to run riot and was never scythed as it was in the early days. But I must say the estate had potential and with more helping hands father could have reaped a harvest.

In the early part of the century, the church was greatly concerned with the evils of drink and held temperance meetings to try and reform the drunkards of the village by getting them to sign the pledge. In those days the social centres were the church gatherings or the public houses. Father thought it best for us to attend church while he frequented the pub. A few pints of beer gave him the Dutch courage to speak his mind, when otherwise he would have remained silent. Such was the case one evening he visited the Wheelwrights Arms (Monkton Combe. Ed.) after which he decided to visit the Fullers Earth Works and take Arthur Gerrish to task over some work he was supposed to do but had not done. Arthur did not take kindly to his remarks and blows were struck, and father came off worse. As well as getting a black eye, the blame for striking the first blow and the sack, and, as the house went with the job, he lost that as well. I thought it was a bit unfair as father was dedicated to his job. Mr Keevil, the manager, said that father had no jurisdiction over the personnel of the works, as he was only their equal, not in any way superior. This was a very queer statement to make as it was obvious someone had to keep an eye on the works and convey orders from the management to the staff. At the time it was very puzzling to me. I felt no animosity towards Arthur, in fact, I thought he was a bit of a hero to give father a thump, something I had always wanted to do myself, but was not big enough to do it.

The next man appointed as foreman (but only equal to the others) was Mr Ernest West of Rock Cottage, Quarry Vale, Combe Down. He had been one of father's mates at the works and a very likable gentleman. Apparently there was not much vacant accommodation available at that time, so the only thing to do was to swap houses. 'Smacker' Gerrish of Combe Down arrived one morning with the first load of furniture in a Sentinel steam lorry, as he unloaded it on to the roadway to be carried into the house, he recounted with some malicious enjoyment the predicament that Mr West found himself in on the journey down the Frome Road by Midford Castle. He was sitting in the back of the lorry when sparks from the smoke stack caught fire to the bedding. At first his cries to Smacker to stop went unheeded owing to the noise of the engine, when eventually the message got through and the lorry stopped, there was quite a blaze to stamp out. Not to have too much on the highway, Smacker flung some of the smaller items over the hedge, mumbling 'mustn't catch'. With one load down and one load up continuing throughout the day, the change over was relatively quick and efficient. By nightfall we found ourselves with our goods and chattels in a dreadful slum, known as Rock Cottage, Quarry Vale, Combe Down. It was detached, but built under a bank that exuded moisture, which made the small backyard and kitchen damp and slimy in places. There were two rooms up and two rooms down, with a central wooden staircase running up from the front door. Sections of the floor were missing from the front room as if the previous tenants had been short of kindling wood. Here all excess baggage was flung in a heap.

The events of the previous days must have been a shock to mother, but she did not complain. During our first month in this dreadful hovel most of the family went down with influenza, and father was out of work with no dole money being paid at that time. However, my elder sister already had a job away from home and I was doing a paper round for Francis Rhymes at three and sixpence a week and getting one and six on the bread round for Hobbs. However, I gave up this lucrative business to take a regular situation at Combe Grove at seven and six and keep for an eighty hour week, obtained for me by Boss Collins, Headmaster of Combe Down School. Then a new sewer trench was required from Combe Down to Bathampton and beyond; this enabled father to get a pick-and-shovel job for a considerable time. The Reverend Warrington then found us a much better house at Mount Pleasant and once more we were back on our feet.

Alas, Tucking Mill has deteriorated, becoming overgrown and squalid. The bridge disgracefully buried up and the right of way along the tow path fenced off. This area of galvanised iron sheeting that was Fullers Earth Works was always an eyesore, but on the whole the valley was picturesque and charming. When revisiting the place I began to envisage a lake instead of the works and a castle shrouded in the mist in the background. Magically, the lake has materialised without any effort from me. All I ask now is, if the glorious S & D is not to be brought back, then use the bricks of the viaduct to build the castle, open up the tow path and put the water back in the canal. I cannot help but wonder how the pattern of life would have changed for me if the events of the last week at Tucking Mill House had not occurred. One thing is certain, *I'll always remember Tucking Mill.*

The 'Bluebell Steps' leading down to Tucking Mill from Summer Lane

Tucking Mill House

Tucking Mill Cottage

Tucking Mill Cottages

Somerset and Dorset Railway tunnel entrance at Lyncombe Vale

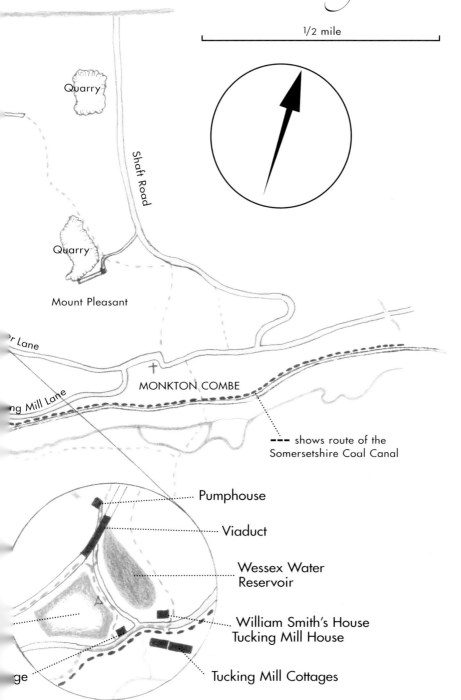

1/2 mile

Quarry

Shaft Road

Quarry

Mount Pleasant

r Lane

ng Mill Lane

MONKTON COMBE

--- shows route of the
Somersetshire Coal Canal

Pumphouse

Viaduct

Wessex Water
Reservoir

William Smith's House
Tucking Mill House

ge

Tucking Mill Cottages

Stanley and friend in Belgium, Nov 1944

Stanley in the garden at Monkswold, 1976

Gwen and Stanley outside the cottage at Mount Pleasant, 1961

Gwen, Carlene, Phillip and Stanley in the garden at Mount Pleasant, 1980

Phillip, Gwen and Stanley outside the cottage at Mount Pleasant, 1984

39

Stanley and Gwen in their garden at Mount Pleasant, 1989

Seven Rambles from Tucking Mill

The walks described by Stanley Wicks are more in the nature of rambles than serious walks; none is more than a mile and a half. Some cross what is now private land, and can not be followed to the letter, unless permission from the land owner is obtained. There is still a good network of public footpaths which follow most of his original walks though one public right of way is currently obstructed. One walk goes along a section of the Limestone Link and a couple go along roads - care must be taken walking along these narrow lanes.

Midford Castle and parkland

The Somersetshire Coal Canal outside Tucking Mill

The Viaduct and fishing lake as it is today

Ramble One~
...Following Horsecombe Brook

Start at the footpath to the left of Tucking Mill Cottage (the house with the William Smith plaque).

From the sparkling spring and Tucking Mill Cottage, come with me towards the railway viaduct and the pump house. Imagine the brown leaves littering the flint road by a walled-up doorway in the wall, then a host of Rhode Island Reds chattering among themselves as they search for titbits among the debris. It is a tranquil scene with nothing to disturb it except, perhaps, the commotion of Mr Hamlen and his six horses drawing a wagon for the fullers earth transportation, a stray dog and the one and only three-wheeled car that may pass through once, now and again. Now as we tread the ash surface of the Back Lane in summer we shall be very conscious of the splendid row of lime trees that grow along the top of the bank of Hamlen's Park on our left. Countless bees buzz around the green blossoms that grow in profusion on the branches and scent the air with a heady redolence. On our right is a hedge mostly of elder that endeavours to shut out the view of the Fullers Earth Works. Soon we are passing the square chimney *(demolished in 1968.Ed)* that is a landmark in the valley. Very soon we are confronted by the giant railway viaduct and the road divides. The one to the left takes us to Midford Castle Park. *(Past the Wessex Water Pump House the path divides - take the left hand path)*.

It is here on the verge of the wood, I found my pet owl when, as I remember, a small group of us were out bird's nesting as usual. In a hole in an old elm tree we thought there was a nest of some description, for we saw a parent bird leave it. I was (tempted?) to attempt the climb, but owing to the many twiggy (growths?) that would not bear your weight, I had to give up. Harold, the next contender, managed to scramble up into the hole. He said excitedly 'I don't see any eggs but there is a bird sitting on the nest'. In actual fact there were two and they were young owls. Startled by the intrusion, they both took off and fluttered to the ground. Dennis Robinson from Combe Down caught one, and I the other. Poor Harold had none, but it did not seem to worry him.

The one Dennis took to Combe Down died the next day, but mine lived on for more than six weeks. I put it in a disused hen house and the parent bird used to answer his plaintive chirp and bring him May bugs and dormice during the night. I was quite proud of him and carried him around on my shoulder. Then one night he disappeared, and I thought he had gone for ever but one day returning from school, mother said 'I've found your owl, the college boys were interested in something in the orchard, I went to investigate and lo and behold it was the owl crouching in the long grass'. Three days after being put back in the hen house, my owl died. The experts said that old birds had been embittered by the imprisonment of their offspring and had poisoned it.

The road to the right now dips down over Horsecombe Brook. Hereabouts I remember one Sunday afternoon a courting couple were walking arm in arm, with Austin Cross and me in close attendance, when the young lady turned and I expected a backhander, but surprise, surprise, she offered me a packet of chocolates or I thought she did. When I went to take it she said 'Oh no, not the whole packet, just one each for you and your friend'.

Someway below this is a fence in a larch wood, cascading from which is a tumbling stream of clear spring water. This meanders towards us down the Springfield, nourishing as it comes, watercress and other water plants and finally disappears under the path into the Pump House.

This section of the path points the way to Horsecombe Bottom. That is to the south west over a combination stile and five-barred gate into a wood, on the left perceive some very marshy land rich in osiers. This could easily be called the valley of the Horsecombe Brook. This runs along the bottom of the extensive Castle Park woodland. From here a steep bank covered in forest trees lead us to a turreted structure with a large banqueting hall on the ground floor, or so it appears as it was said that after a grand hunt in the forest, some sort of revelry went on here. In my day, the outside of the building was intact, but the roof and upper floors of the tower had fallen away. Countless feet have climbed the spiral staircase as countless names are inscribed on the walls, give ample evidence to the fact. We kids scrambled all over it, even round the top where the roof was missing, clinging on to the ramparts and digging our toes in the remaining lead work while looking down forty feet to the basement. I remember placing a penny in a matchbox, hiding it in the ivy around there, and daring anybody to retrieve it. Somebody did and I was a penny poorer. Growing near the building you may see several lady chestnut trees, but the small nuts in the prickly cases that strew the ground are hardly worth considering as the nut is inferior.

Going back to the track through the wood, I remember a small cave that seemed to be filling up with debris from above. This is on the right side and is a bank of various trees interspersed with thorny undergrowth. Above and beyond this section of the woods, is an airy plain dotted with oak trees. Continuing our way westward along a muddy track, we find our way barred by another gate and stile combination. Then across some grassland and through another barrier into a wood that seems to join together the Beech Wood of Combe Down and the Castle Woods of Midford.

Here the Horsecombe Brook idles its way through a flat portion of the woods. On the right hand side the bank of trees stretch away upward to Shepherd's Gate and Summer Lane. The brook passes under the path, if the pipe is not blocked up at the next gate and stile, here too we shall see evidence of the fullers earth pipeline to Tucking Mill as it appears on the surface as the grassland of Horsecombe Bottom begins. Here in my early years in the mist of early morning, I would stand here with some friends and scan the green swards for the sign of a white blob that could possibly be a mushroom, for here they grew in late summer. There was always some rivalry between us, and our unknown competitors who would sometimes rise from their beds a little earlier and gather the crop before we got there. The brook follows the bottom of the Beech Wood towards Glasshouse and The Pan.

(The public footpath now divides, turn left to join Midford Road or right through the Beech Wood to Combe Down. Stanley Wicks was able to follow the brook up to the top of Horsecombe Vale - now partly accessible in the Right to Roam area.)

About half way along the meadow, in the field opposite a large beech tree, I remember a large fire built in the 1914 war years to consume a herd of cattle that suffered from foot and mouth disease. As we reach the trees at the end of the pasture land, we see a useful orchard on the right hand bank, known to us kids and visited on convenient occasions. Over a stile crowded with thorny bushes, we come to The Pan and a trolley way of iron rails leading to the top of the slope.

We went to the ground at the top of Combe Hay Lane where father forked out sixpence for him and three pence for me to get in. Then he found out that the team we had come to watch, Monkton Rovers, were playing at the playing fields near the Red Lion. Luckily here they were only making a collection, or father could have gone broke. Our trip then, along Horsecombe Brook to its source which was a spring in the bank near The Pan, is finished. Should we wish to return to Tucking Mill another way, we could do this by way of Combe Down or Midford.

Ramble Two~

... From the Somerset & Dorset railway viaduct to Combe Down

Start at the same place as Ramble One up to the viaduct.

To ramble further in Tucking Mill let us return to the Somerset and Dorset railway viaduct, a place of blue violets and wild strawberries. We now turn under the railway viaduct and as it curves to the right we see the Pump House set in behind ornate flower beds and pebble paths. The flower beds were filled with pinks in Summertime and the pumps throbbed away under the loving care of Roly Bishop of Combe Down and Tom Hamlen of Monkton Combe. Tom was nicknamed 'Rattler' and was a great character, a member of the family of Hamlen of Midford. He would walk Tucking Mill Lane daily, usually carrying a tin on a wire to transport oily waste that had polished the gas engines at the Pump House and was destined to light the fire in his house near the church.

From the Pump House the track narrows, and changes from ash to yellow clay, and goes up a small rise, following the railway; ahead is a gate and a stile, on the other side of which is Springfield. The railway embankment diminishes and a cutting appears just before Combe Down Tunnel, from there a swing gate will give you access to the Bluebell Steps. To the left of which can be seen the slim chimney of the old Cabinet Works *(De Montalt Mill. Ed.)*

The brick walls bordering the track were a direct challenge to us boys, ultimate and death defying, who could walk along the parapet farthest before jumping down on the track. The secret was not to look down the hundred foot drop to the Horsecombe Brook. Nobody ever got more than a quarter way across and nobody ever made the big drop.

If we climb the embankment at the tunnel we may see the site of the railway station that never was - the railway planners were a bit optimistic and besides widening the viaduct to put in a double track, they made provision for a station here just outside the tunnel should the populace get enthusiastic and flock in their thousands down Bluebell Steps in order to travel by rail to the seaside. This did not happen so more cash had gone down the drain.

Walk up the Bluebell Steps, cross Summer Lane taking the drung almost opposite, up to Combe Down Village.

A steam train emerging from the Combe Down Tunnel

Ramble Three~
... Tucking Mill to Summer Lane

So, on our magic carpet back to Tucking Mill to explore the Paddock; usually a paddock is known for horses, but for some reason this path was called the Paddock, so the Paddock it shall be. It starts at the roadside near Tucking Mill House *(on the right of the house. Ed.)* You will see on the right hand side a veritable cliff covered with trees and bushes, among them I remember a luscious plum tree, very few knew of it but I sampled its fruit year by year. On the other side a snowberry hedge follows the path to Tucking Mill House where it gives way to mainly ivy. Near the house in the bank is a nice cave hewn out of the yellowish rock - we kids spent quite a lot of time in there digging in the sand. I wonder if William Smith the Father of English Geology, did likewise in his time. A little further up is a lesser cave.

Above the two caves is a path that can take you back along the cliff top to the middle of Tucking Mill Hill. Beyond the second cave was a the uphill entrance to Number One Orchard. At the top of this is a narrow strip of woodland, mostly of elm, really an extension of the hedge. This greenery, when viewed from Summer Lane, is the borderline between the farm lands of Monkton Combe and the Fullers Earth Works estate.

The apple trees in Number One Orchard were poor and the fruit small and sour. Despite this the apples were eaten by us although we were inviting stomach ache. I remember one day father speaking like a parent of Kung Fu, saying to me 'Go, my son to the entrance to Number One Orchard, me thinks I see a rabbit in a snare'. I did as I was bidden and sure enough at the entrance of the orchard was a dead rabbit with its head in a snare. Then something shining in the stubble of the recently mown grass attracted my attention. It was an Ingersol watch, one that you can see in the dark. It was indeed a treasure - it must have cost all of five shillings. I carried the rabbit back to father and showed him the watch. I was allowed to keep it. Periodically, it would stop until I washed it out with paraffin, then off it would go again. The Ingersol went for years and nobody ever claimed it.

Looking south-west from this vantage point, you get the best panoramic view that is obtainable of the Fullers Earth Works estate. Here on the downward slope is an apple tree that used to shed its fruit in a secret sort of way, and if the apples did not roll to the bottom of the incline, they remained hidden in the long tufty grass and became a storehouse for apple-eating mice. Such as I would get the urge to ferret them out, sometimes as late as December. It was here beneath this apple tree that mother found my lost owl, which reminds me of another bird that gained our attention.

It was in the thicket, on the upper side of the Paddock, in the brushwood at the base of a small wych elm. A nightingale had built a nest of leaves and therein were four olive green eggs. Now for some reason we kids had respect for the nightingale, but our desire to add this rare specimen to our tatty egg collections, was overwhelming. After a discussion, we decided to take just one egg for all to be able to view in years to come. However, the bird who sang so beautifully between April and June did not like the intrusion and deserted the nest. Of course when we were sure that this had happened we had a good excuse to take the rest of the eggs. Despite our ill-treatment of the songster, the nightingales came every spring and their amazing song would trill through the woods of the valley of Tucking Mill.

De Montalt mill and chimney (far left)

49

As we proceed now, the trees close in on both sides, and on the right of this is an upward path to Number Two Orchard. (*This footpath to Summer Lane is currently obstructed so you are obliged to go up the Bluebell Steps. Turn right down Summer Lane to view Kingham Quarry on the left. Ed.*)

To some old quarry workings. (*These could be William Smith's Kingham Quarry. There was a tramway to take stone down to Tucking Mill, following the path of the Bluebell Steps, where William Smith had a stone sawing mill in the very early years of the 1800s. Ed.*). Here the trees are tall, allowing the dampness of air to colour the stone a dingy yellow, quite unlike the stone used in the houses of Tucking Mill. If the stone was not used in this way, what was the purpose of the quarry?

I have good reason to remember this neck of the woods. Along the top of the quarry runs a very narrow path, and when I was very young, I remember negotiating this veritable goat track one morning with Alec Palmer. At one difficult root-ridden bit, Alec suddenly decided to forge ahead, and as he scrambled by, threw me off my balance and I went over the cliff. I suppose there was a drop of fifteen feet, but luckily the continual fall of debris that was eroded from the wooden slope above, created a shelving bank below, on which I landed. I was unhurt, apart from an abrasion on my forehead, that trickled blood into my eye. This frightened me as I thought I was bleeding to death, but it did not stop me from running home to mother who bathed the wound and said I would live. I was rather pleased to find that Alec was concerned at my welfare and had followed me down to get the verdict.

Alec featured in another episode in the Paddock, near the quarry. Like all kids, we had been in the habit of copying the grown-ups and had taken to smoking. Not tobacco, we had no money for that, but pieces of dead old man's beard, when lit up, it would smoke just like a cigarette - but very acrid. One morning, like a magician, Alec produced a packet of ten Players from his pocket. He offered me one, put one in his own mouth, and lit the two with one match, just like grown-ups. I puffed away, feeling at least ten years older, until I began to feel decidedly ill and became very sick - and gave up smoking for good.

In the quarry itself, I well remember out hunting with father one Saturday. We had already caught five rabbits simply by covering up all the burrows of a rabbit warren with nets and putting a ferret down one of them. Rabbits do not like ferrets for a very good reason and run for their lives to the outside world. Of course when they get there, they find themselves entangled in a string net and that is usually the finish of them.

Here by the quarry was a huge burrow, almost a small cave, and father had to drape the net over the boulders to secure it. The ferret went in and almost immediately there was a drumming of scurrying feet and a rabbit virtually shot out of the burrow with such force that it knocked the net off the boulders and carried it at least six feet. It was my job to pounce on the poor creature and hang on until father came to dispatch it with a karate chop, only I managed to grab the net and the rabbit struggled free. Of course father said 'Don't grab the net, my son, get hold of the rabbit'. He was not too perplexed for, after all, at the end of the day we had caught six.

I am told there are sixty one Bluebell Steps, not counting a few at the bottom. In the old days, we climbed this stairway most days to attend school *(Combe Down Old School in Church Road. Ed.)*, after the age of eleven, having spent our earlier years at Monkton Combe.

Such characters as old Fred came down those steps carrying a large basket on his arm covered with a sack which. when lifted, would reveal a few bloaters, a few pairs of kippers or some yellow haddock. One day Fred arrived at our house and the conversation went like this: 'Good morning, Mam. Would you like a nice piece of haddock, a pair of kippers or a couple of bloaters?' Mother:'My husband said that the bloaters you brought last week were gone off'. Fred: 'Your husband would grumble, if he had to be hung'. Mother: 'Wouldn't you then?'. Fred: 'Not if I'd dunnit.' Fred had made his point and mother, duly impressed, found another four pence for two bloaters, and Fred went away happy.

I can also recall the day that mother had to take my elder sister to the Royal United Hospital to have her tonsils removed. It meant the long haul up the Bluebell Steps and a journey on the tramcar to the hospital. A long wait for mother in the waiting room for the patient to gain consciousness after the operation and the long journey back. My sister was on the point of collapse and had to be carried across the fields and down the Paddock to Tucking Mill House where the Palmers were still in residence. Here she was revived and later taken down to the cottages.

Later on when we actually took up residence in Tucking Mill House, I remember the occasion when my brother was coughing fit to choke. Mother became alarmed and telephoned Doctor Morris of Combe Down. It was a quarter to twelve on a very stormy night when he arrived. I remember it well, he was arrayed in a dark overcoat and a black bowler hat all glistening in the lamplight with moisture. He administered some kind of jollop from a brown leather case and said to mother 'I am not well myself, Mrs Wicks, the child has only got a cold and you have fetched me out of a warm bed to treat him, across those muddy fields in such atrocious weather'. Such was the dedication of old Doctor Morris.

I, too, made many journeys up and down the Bluebell Steps. I remember during the six weeks summer holidays, climbing up there to the school gardens to apply liquid manure to the parsnips and the beans. Austin and myself were partners on the plot, and were in the running for the distinction of having the best plot. Of course, I was in the position of being able to obtain the best bean sticks and the nice twiggy pea sticks. This helped the appearance of the lot no end. I think eventually we failed on the written part and came second. I also featured in the basket-carrying marathon when I worked for Hobbs the Baker. With delectable cakes, buns and bread covered with a flour sack, I delivered to the farm down the Bluebell Steps and to Tucking Mill on Saturdays in all winds and weather. I was accused of pinching the weekly bread money amounting to one and sixpence half penny. Mrs Dudley at the farm said she would give me a chance to own up and cough up. Mother immediately took me to the shop where the good Mrs Hobbs took the blame saying she had omitted to cross it off the book, so ended a storm in a teacup.

Summer Lane, 1900s

Ramble Four~
... Tucking Mill Cottages to Midford by road

Our next walk might as well be along Midford Lane. With white-painted railings bordering the canal on our left, and a wall supporting the Park on our right, you may be able to locate a beech tree that was a mere sapling in the twenties. Here in the topmost branches we built a crow's nest, and on a Sunday evening lay in wait for Mr Stockley, an elderly gentleman and devout chapel goer respected by all who knew him. As he passed on his way to Midford we would endeavour to pour water from a bottle on his best Sunday hat. He would look up in a friendly way, waggle his finger at us and say 'I know you are up there'.

The road turns up a a small slope with trees and bushes with a carpet of onion-smelling ramsons at the base. On the right is a bank surmounted by a hedge with some elm trees behind in a row reaching along to where the railway embankment nearly reaches the road. Here is a place of evil-smelling mud as a small spring dampens the neighbourhood as the beasts from the pasture come to drink. A quickset hedge now borders the canal side, and a wall takes over on the right and another piece of Hamlen's Park is revealed.

As we approach Midford Hill, the place where Mr Hamlen used to whip up his six horses to breast the slope to the siding, there is a five-barred gate in the wall and beyond this on the rising ground was a chestnut tree. Here we were frequent visitors in the conker season - here was the place that my brother learned for the first time the laws of gravity: what goes up must come down. Here he collected a good size flint on the head, one that was destined to bring down some conkers, but didn't.

The canal now turns away from us as we attack the hill with the railway siding on our right with a branch road leading into it. Midford Lane continues between two high banks surmounted by hazel bushes. Here I remember the intrepid Bill Norris riding down here at a fair pace with four up. One on the handlebars, one on the bar, one on the saddle and one on the carrier. As we reach the top end of the siding there is a weigh engine, where Hamlens used to weigh the coal and on the same side, over the wall, was a lean-to for pigs. Now ahead of us the road goes over the railway. We kids used to stand above the arch over the line, and gaze in wonder as the trains rushed by in a flurry of steam and sparks.

On the left used to be a signal and a good view of this section of the line as it reaches Midford Station. On top of the hill to our right we get a sparkling view of Midford Castle. We are now approaching what used to be the horse stables, with a strip of grassland on the left and a park with sycamore trees on the right. I remember the days when, with a small pair of trucks fitted with pram wheels and with the aid of a shovel, I was collecting horse manure from the roadway for the garden. So far I had not been successful in my quest, but when reaching the stables, I was invited in by Walter Hamlen and presented by several very damp dollops from the stalls. I thought at the time that Walter was treating the event with some subdued hilarity, not without good reason, for I had not progressed very far on my return journey, when the pram wheels folded up under the box. I therefore separated the transport from the compost and dragged the wreckage home rewardless.

Midford view showing Midford Station and Canal Weigh House

Beyond the stables at the cross roads, the Old Post Office, now the House of Hamlen, on the other side I remember a dairy. Down the steep hill from the cross roads, on the left hand side is the Midford Chapel. It was early in life that I attended Chapel here. I understand that the reason for going to Midford was because there were no older children to take us to Monkton Combe. Here at Midford, Vera Morris officiated at the harmonium and three venerable gentlemen ran the evening service. They were Messrs Larcombe, Landsdowne and Stephens. I vividly remember one such service, during a long-winded diatribe by Mr Lansdowne, I had been snatching sweets across the aisle from a friend on the other side, causing some subdued giggling, and some kids in the second front row had been so bored that they had taken to playing Put and Take on the floor. When the sermon at last came to an end, Mr Stephens stalked to the front of the hall, livid with pent-up emotion. He said in a tense voice 'I have never in my long association with this Chapel, seen such disgraceful goings on during a religious address, and if it happens again I shall disassociate myself forever from this Chapel.' What he said was away above our heads but infinitely more interesting than what had gone before.

A little farther down the hill was a thatched cottage overlooking the railway. It was here many years ago a group of us, a few days before Christmas, decided to render *Christmas Awake* in hope of monetary gain. We had hardly got started when to our surprise a gentleman come to the door with his collar on backward and a finger to his lips. He ushered us into his warm kitchen and gave us warm milk and three pence, and implored us not to sing any more as they just got the baby to sleep. It was obvious that he did not look on the row we kicked up as a lullaby. We left the premises very quietly and set off for Midford Castle.

A few days days earlier, I had gone up to the Castle with Bill Morris to return a crosscut saw. It had been impressed upon us by Bill's father that Mr Epworth liked being called Major, and making use of the fact might loosen up the Major's purse strings. In fact we were rewarded with three pence. So, in the semi-darkness of a December evening, suitably illuminated by our candle lantern, a small group of us started to sing in the forecourt of Midford Castle. Almost immediately the Major came to the door and flung us a three penny bit, we all said 'Thank you, Major', stopped singing, and hunted through the gravel for the coin. The Major said ' Don't worry about the coin - go on singing'. This we did, but not for long; the Major must have been disenchanted by our melodious voices for, after tossing us another coin, he went in and shut the door.

Somersetshire Coal Canal outside Tucking Mill

Ramble Five~
... Tucking Mill to Midford along the former canal

At Tucking Mill House the public footpath from Combe Down crosses the road going westwards and is diverted over a stile following the north bank of Midford Brook - this is part of the Limestone Link footpath.

We shall learn more in the way of a canal if we return to Tucking Mill Bridge and travel south-west. Straight away we view the extensive meadow land set between the line of trees that mark the meandering brook and the walled embankment that supports the towpath and the canal. As we start our walk, we see the final flow of the Horsecombe Book as it surges out of the bank beneath us. The next item of interest is the hazel tree growing in the left hand bank; this has given a crop of nuts for as long as I can remember and still does. The canal now passes the old wharf to the spring, where I remember the stream in the middle being bridged by a plank to enable a fisherman and bathers to get across dry footed to the brook area. This was a path used by people from Combe Down and even Bath, by way of the Paddock to get to the Midford Brook.

One such visitor was Mr Watson who had a cobbler's shop in Widcombe; he used to get me to dig worms for him to bait his hooks. I was sometimes rewarded with a small trout. I don't think he really came to fish - he probably liked the solitude of the river bank. The meadow was a place of buttercups and daisies, dandelions and cowslips. A place to lie and listen to the buzz of the bees collecting nectar from the blossoms and to watch the clouds go by in the summer. In winter it was sometimes flooded and the gasping moles, or 'wants' as father used to call them, swam in panic from their flooded underground houses, sometimes to be clubbed to death for their pelts.

Now on the wall of the meadow is a spreading wych elm a great favourite for climbing; we used to sit in the branches like a lot of chattering monkeys, eating our tea - it always tasted better that way. The usual menu was slices of bread spread with cocoa butter, a concoction of margarine, cocoa and sugar. I don't remember any tea; we must have settled for a swig out of the spring.

The canal now bends with the road towards the west and the herbage in the canal is quite fantastic. Beside the reeds are bullrushes, hog weed, comfrey, horsetails, hemlock, meadow sweet and a host of others. On the right bank of the canal is a place of ramsons and tangled vines of blackberry and old man's beard - and bird life. The retaining bank of the towpath following the fringe of the meadow is also supporting a large number of small elm trees. The canal now veers more southward and in the meadow adjacent to the wall there is a tall ash tree that has lost a lower limb and a hole in the trunk has resulted. Here, year after year, a pair of starlings have made a nest and raised a noisy brood. Nails driven into the truck and a pile of stones at the base is clear evidence of our endeavours to look into the nesting place. However, the starlings remained unmolested; we were never clever enough to scale the tree. Hereabouts was a place of hayricks and horse mushrooms. These fungi were big as dinner plates and edible but not at all palatable.

There is now a straight portion of towpath, and for a while, the the retaining wall disappears and a boundary wall sort of emerges from the depths of the meadow to the top of the terrain. We are now approaching the section of the canal near the bottom of Midford Hill, just below the siding. Here there was always a rough track across the waterway to communicate the road with the towpath. In line with it was a culvert under the path in the form of a tunnel, for the purpose of draining the water of the canal into the brook should the need arise. We kids, invariably had to investigate the tunnel if we came this way. I remember a stile into the meadow, and a group of maple trees as the canal bends slightly westwards, and a steep wooded bank appears on the Midford Hill side. This props up a strip of pasture land, and the road which now edges continually toward the railway and then passes over it. The canal bank now supports the rail track as the canal curves southerly below the Midford Station.

On the brook side is a mass of blackthorn, remembered for the long-tailed tit's nest that was always there in early summer. Exquisitely built of lichen in the form of a ball, with a hole in the side, and lined with feathers. It was always just out of our reach on a sloping bank. Just opposite in the bed of the canal was a ghastly structure of galvanised metal sheets with points on the top that protected a sewer of all things.

The towpath retaining wall is now almost on the bank of the brook and here is a hawthorn tree noted for the fact that mistletoe grows on its lower branches. Below the hawthorn tree is a delightful spring that must have been used by the early residents of Midford for drinking water. On the right below the railway station is the

Midford Weigh House post 1874

site of the old barge weighing machine, which had the appearance of a Greek temple with stone pillars *(built in 1831 and demolished in 1914. Ed.)*. The staff cottage is still there and I remember a Mr Steger living there who was one of the officials who did the weighing.

Nearby can still be seen the tunnel under the Frome Road, which carried the canal onward to a parting of the ways; where one arm goes through a series of locks to the coal field and the other crosses the right arm of the brook, which also divides, and joins a tramway coming down the hill, also from the coal fields. Of late years, land owners have tried to block the pathway but not completely succeeded. You can still get through to Frome Road and Rose Cottage, which no longer sells sweets like Mrs Bath used to do in the twenties.

I remember when in a terrific thunderstorm a tree was struck by lightening on the hillside above the Hamlen farm buildings at the bottom of the road to Limpley Stoke. We hurried along the towpath from Tucking Mill knowing the general direction of the occurrence, and all excited, thinking we were going to dig up an actual thunderbolt when no such thing exists. Mr Walter said the cows were so frightened, as it happened at milking time, that one of them put her foot in the milk pail and upset it. Mr Geoff Evans who was standing under the bridge carrying the Great Western line when the lightening flash rendered him helpless for minutes. I remember the wetness of the grass, the strip of bark torn from the trunk of the elm tree, and the loud twittering of the birds who seemed to burst forth into vigorous song after the storm that had cooled their ardour early on.

Tucking Mill canal bridge

Ramble Six~

...Tucking Mill to Monkton Combe by road with a detour to Limpley Stoke

From Tucking Mill Canal Bridge, we start up the hill; almost at once the memory comes flooding back of the wasp nest in the light brown sandy bank on the left hand side. Arthur Gerrish and his two pals, Sid and Percy Harris - sons of the decorator who rented the ponies field - were armed with a spade. Arthur took the first dig while his friends, with suitable leafy branches, endeavoured to keep the wasps at bay. It only needed one dig and the wasps came out in droves and attacked their persecutors. Arthur flung down the spade and took to his heels, away down toward the Fullers Earth Works, shedding his clothes as he ran. Having reached the spring and freedom from the wasps, he cautiously returned to pick up his coat and waistcoat and shake out the wasps. We kids thought this was good entertainment and and were sorry it was so short lived.

Half way up the hill by a stone and a tree in the top of the bank, an event occurred that still puzzles me. I was proceeding upward with Austin when we saw Noel Kearns and his nanny approaching from the opposite direction. We were about to pass when Noel attacked and kicked me on the leg. I was amazed. I had not provoked him in any way. I had just got over the initial shock, and thought about giving him one back, when his nanny intervened and dragged him away. I never felt so innocent in my life; the blame lay entirely with the Headmaster's son. Next day, they admitted it, for Noel and his nanny arrived at the cottage bearing a gift of chocolate and Noel was made to apologise. It was a small package of very thin bars, but very acceptable. So much so that I was ready to be kicked on the leg every day providing I got the chocolate. There seemed to be a scarcity of this commodity at Tucking Mill.

One day I had visited Limpley Stoke railway station and saw people getting chocolate from a slot machine by inserting a coin. This set me thinking: if a copper coin produced the chocolate, then any other metal would do the same. So one day I got hold of an aluminium disc from a tin of Bournville cocoa and decided to make the trip to Limpley Stoke. One morning bright and early, four of us set off along Tucking Mill Lane, through the village and down over Tynee, a field near the college, over the railway and along the road by the cricket field, under the eleven arches and along the Lower Stoke Road to the station. We gathered expectantly around the machine as I looked round to see if anybody was looking, then satisfied that nobody was interested in our escapade, I took the disc from my pocket and inserted it in to the slot. Now came the crunch - would the drawer come out, that was the question. I pulled. It was coming but then stuck half way. Should I dig out the chocolate with a pocket knife, it was just visible? Should I be bold and return the drawer to its former position, and then give it an almighty tug - it was bound to come out that way? I was wrong, it went back in and no amount of pulling would get it out again. As it happened, nobody took any notice of our manoeuvres, had they done so, they might have been sympathetic and supplied us with a real penny. You can imagine what a dispirited group left that railway station and wended their way back home. I remember it seemed so much longer than the inward trip.

However, let us proceed a little further up the hill to the tree and the stone near the road. Down over the bank is a smooth slope down which we used to slide on old baking tins from the tip, wearing great holes in our trousers in the process. Near the slide is a beech tree with crossed branches on which, one year, there was a mistle thrush's nest. It was infuriating that we could not get up there without a long ladder, an object rarely seen in Tucking Mill.

A little further up the hill, looking down the bank, there is a tall slim beech that I could climb. If you go to the top, you will find my initials carved in the trunk dated 1921. My next landmark up the hill is an oak on the same side and reminds me of a school song and it goes like this

> *The old oak stands and stretches out his hands,*
> *by the side of the rolling river*
> *And the branches sway as the wind goes by that way,*
> *and delicate leaflets quiver*
> *Alas no more in Spring will its budding branches swing,*
> *neath the fleecy clouds above him*
> *For the woodmen came and cut him down,*
> *and we grieve for we used to love him.*

It had a nice little tune worth bringing back to the public's attention.

Now on the left hand side is a retaining wall and a track to the ploughed field beyond. Here in a group are larch trees that have small red flowers in spring and pleasantly scent the air as you go past. The trees nearest to the ploughed field cling precariously to the top of the bank, and in doing so create a small cave in the bank supported by their roots. Here I remember crawling in with a few companions and starting a small fire with twigs and dry leaves just in time to attract the attention of the arm of the law who came pedalling into view on his bike. He dismounted with great purpose and put his bike against the bank, and said 'Hallo, what's going on here?' With great authority, he read us the realm act about endangering other people's property and told us to put the fire out immediately. This did not require much effort for we had great difficulty in keeping it alight. We kids had great fear of the police - if you did anything wrong you were threatened by 'I'll tell your mother, your father' and, the ultimate: 'I'll tell the policeman.' In this instance I was selected as the ringleader and my father was instructed to give me a hiding. Father did not like the law and resented being told how to bring up his family - I got off without even a telling off.

So on to the level at the top of the hill; there was always a heap of flints for road repair and nearby was our number one rubbish heap. Periodically transport would arrive and there was a tuneful rattle as the tins and bottles cascaded down the bank. This would fetch us from our haunts to hunt through the new consignment for useful oddments like tins for swimming, bits of timber for trolleys and bottles for smashing. A few yards farther on is a more select tip, this one was called the Hole, as it was a hole in the bank, and here one day I found in the grass a sixpenny piece, rather worn, with a picture of Queen Victoria on it. I picked it up conjuring up visions of all the good things I could get for it at Plummer's sweet shop. Then Bill Norris spoilt everything by coming in announcing that it was his - he had just dropped it. I believed him and gave him the tanner.

The two rubbish heaps are in an area of woodland on a bank between the canal and the road and is dotted with trees and undergrowth that reaches from the bridge to the Great Western Railway. We call it the 'Brake' and there are several paths that allow passage through it. During the 1914 war there were many sham flights *(or fights? Ed.)* here, and the area was strewn with spent cartridge cases.

The road runs now between two mossy banks for a time until iron railings take over on the Brake side. On the left, the bank diminishes and a hedge takes us to a five-barred gate. Here is a place for hayricks, marigolds and scarlet pimpernels. The hedgerow becomes elder and later turns to a conglomeration of hawthorn, blackberry, old man's beard and stinging nettles. With a hedge of hazels we came to the end of the Brake, although it is extended by the canal. Now there is a strip of sloping rugged pasture land, and it continues at varying widths to Monkton Combe.

For a while the railings stand alone between the road and the grassland and a view can be had of the old route of the canal, and where the Great Western Railway hoves into view over a bridge from Midford and makes use of its bed to reach Mill Lane Station, and on to Limpley Stoke. Beyond the railway is the brook and Kennel Farm. Here, by these railings the road gets very hot in summer and the hot air can be seen as it shimmers over the flints. This is a place of snakes, flying ants, and other creepy crawlies.

Homeward bound on this stretch of the highway one late afternoon, I was ruminating on what the school teacher had said in the morning lesson; something about the dense clouds of volcanic dust over Vesuvius turning the sky to lurid colours of red, yellow and purple just before Pompeii was destroyed by the debris of the mountain. Looking toward the setting sun, I noticed that the clouds were lurid shades of red, yellow and purple, and I remembered she also said that Bath was built on a sleeping volcano - I knew I was for it. Bath was erupting and I had better get home quickly. But nothing came of it and I lost faith in teachers.

Let us continue along the Lane of so many memories. As the railings come to an end, three ash trees rear up in the hedgerow, two on the left side and one on the right. Almost as if at one time of the hedge's life, someone had decided for some reason to spare some upstanding saplings and ever afterwards allowed them to grow while other twiggy grow was slaughtered back without mercy. I dare say, while the farmer had intended the hedge to be quickset hawthorn, other varieties had crept in, no doubt dispensed by birds wiping their beaks as they are prone to do, and the hedge ends up with a mixture of maple, dogwood, spindleberry, elm, hazel, old man's beard, blackberry, ash and elder, with a generous supply of bryony, convolvulos and stinging nettles. A grand conglomeration to give you the music of Tucking Mill Lane.

In summer the stridations of countless grasshoppers intermingled with the cry of 'little-bit-of-bread-and-no-cheese' from several colourful

Canal Cottage, Monkton Combe where Isaac Owen, Stanley's grandfather lived

yellowhammers. When the wheat was ripe in the cornfield, flocks of marauding sparrows would land in the hedge, give a burst of chirps and be gone again. Among the buttercups, celandines, daisies, cinquefoils, plantains, mallows, dandelions, ragged robins and jack-by-the-hedge that grew on the road verges, were docks to assuage the suffering of those who had been stung by the nettles. The poisonous hemlock grew in profusion everywhere and I remember a lady who was collecting some of it in a basket, warned us to leave it alone as it would make us ill.

In summer, the hedges were industriously searched for bird's nests. When one was located, everybody had to look, thereby trampling down verdure in the immediate vicinity of the nest and gave ample evidence it was there. I often wondered why the birds bothered to build, there was little chance that anything would come of it.

On past the ash trees, round a slight corner, the road dips down a small slope and sweeps round a curve toward Orchard Hill. At the bottom of the slope on the right hand side is an old stunted ash tree. I well remember Bill Morris collecting a group of us very young kids together in a single file on the left hand side at the top of the slope, and in a dramatic voice he cried 'When I give the word run like hell past the Old Man's Tree'. For that is what we called it. As we raced past the Old Man's Tree, there was a blood curdling yell from that direction leaving us rather breathless and excited. We were not brave enough to go back to investigate. The funny thing was, that there was never any old man there unless Bill Morris was around.

On the bend in the road there are more ash trees to mark the corner and a hedge completely of elm commences on the right hand side. Here I remember the road repair men. First of all a machine drawn by a steamroller with crude chunky points loosened up the surface, then freshly broken flints were spread over the prepared area, the water cart sprayed water over it, then the mighty steamroller went to work and crushed and flattened the flints to make a good surface.

Now the road bends upward abruptly round a corner to Orchard Hill; here many things happened to me long years ago. One morning I was going to school in company with most of the pupils from Tucking Mill. We were holding hands across the road, as we approached the corner Jack Bolton came round it at speed on his bike and took me amidships and deposited me in the gutter. Many faces were concerned at my fate and many hands reached down to pull me from the hedgerow, It was a bit of a fright but I was quite unharmed, attired as I was in my seafaring jersey and my sailor's hat. I could not escape the catastrophe as my companions, two on either side, suddenly realised the danger, and set on getting me out of the way, pulled with equal force in opposite directions, thereby presenting me to the front wheel of the bike. Jack Bolton, a very relieved man went on his way home. My sister, Gwendoline, convinced that I was dead and nothing could be done about it, went on to school. When asked by the governess as to my whereabouts, said she did not know.

Over the wall in the churchyard, near Orchard Hill in the grass could be found little mossy hillocks which were the nests of bumble bees. Inside the nests could be had, if you were lucky, some honeycomb, fashioned like a cluster of hazel nuts. We would take out the comb when the owner had buzzed off and sample its sweetness. I don't remember seeing such nests since.

At this time the Church farm had been taken over by farmer Shute from farmer Plaister. One day I was standing on the verge at the bottom of Orchard Hill when there was a thunder of hoofs and grinding of wheels on the flint road, and two horses pulling a wagon of hay came charging along the flat in an endeavour to mount the hill. With farmer Shute cracking his whip and shouting encouragement, they rounded the corner and attacked the gradient, but the farmer had overestimated the power of his steeds and they faltered in the middle of the hill, stopped, and were being dragged backward by the weight of the load. Farmer Shute, a churchgoer and God fearing man, whipped and swore at those horses, and his assistant, poor Jack, also came under the lash of his tongue. The wagon had now come to rest wedged against a wall of the churchyard. Jack was dispatched to the farmyard to obtain a stout post to jam in the wheel to slow the wagon to the bottom of the slope. Jack returned with a stick covered in cow dung, the only one he could find, and stuck it through the wheel spokes. The operation in reverse to the bottom of the hill was started, the farmer shouting and cursing at the horses heads, eased the wagon from the wall. Momentarily, the wagon straightened out in line with the hedge, and the progress down the slope commenced. Then the stick broke, and with the farmer stepping up his flow of lurid language, and the horses trying desperately to keep their feet, the load of hay began to run away, dragging the horses with it. The bank arrested their progress and surprisingly the horses were not injured or any hay dislodged. The perspiring farmer relaxed before deciding to go through the gate by the bottom orchard and put the hay in the big barn.

Another day I was coming through the churchyard gate with my friend Harold, when two lads of about our age from Combe Down, without any preamble said 'What was it you said about me last Friday?' This was the usual ploy to get things started. While I was giving the situation some consideration, Harold was taking the first blow in the chest, but he put his assailant down with an uppercut to the jaw. I hadn't a clue what the fight was about and was beginning to think I ought to give a hand, but I need not have bothered for Harold, getting the swing of things, put the other fellow on the ground. Harold brushed himself down and we resumed our walk towards Tucking Mill. Harold did not explain and I never did find out what that fight was about. He was more interested in camping out, and that is what we intended to do.

Yet another incident occurred on Orchard Hill. It was a Sunday evening in September when all good people were supposed to be in church. Harold, myself and brother Philip were intent on stealing farmer Shute's apples from the top orchard. Previously we had flung bits of sticks and stones from the road at the trees in hope of dislodging a few juicy pippins, so we could venture in the orchard to pick them up. This had always alerted the farmer with the noise we kicked up, so this evening I had decided to do it the scientific way, which was to open the gate and walk in as if you owned the place, then climb up the tree in a civilised sort of way and pick the best fruit. What could be easier? The venture was highly successful and I returned to my colleagues with my pockets full. I shared out the apples as we reached the cross roads with Summer Lane, I then suddenly realised that I had a perfectly good apple core in my hand. Now, apple cores were for throwing, and out of the gloom appeared the faces of three College boys. At the time class distinction was almost painful, and to get back at the ruling class who thought you were less than dust, was highly desirable. Therefore, the middle one received the juicy core straight between the eyes. Momentarily shocked, the unlucky one said 'Where is the cowardly swine', but I had faded into the night across the ploughed field and my colleagues said, truthfully, they had no knowledge of my whereabouts.

At the top of Orchard Hill on May the first, I remember sitting on the bank at eleven o'clock at night eating cream biscuits, a large tin of these comestibles had been presented to us by Mrs Picairn of Bushey House. A group of us, under the direction of Ruby Palmer, danced round the May Pole outside all the big houses to collect money for the hospital, and here we were after a hard day. As we crunched away at the biscuits, the lightening flickered over Hinton Charterhouse and there was a loud sound of thunder. in the distance. Then Father arrived from the Wheelwright's and said 'Hurry along home now there is a storm coming up'. He was right, although we hurried, big drops of rain were falling before we reached the cottage and a good old storm followed that lasted quite a time.

Bushey is the lower hillside encircled by Shaft Road. There was another gracious lady that lived there, her name was Miss Knott. On May the twenty-fourth the pupils would attend school only to sing patriotic songs, and at eleven o'clock were allowed to go home. Each one who went through the front door to the street was given an orange and a bag of bullseyes from two sacks - this was a gift from Miss Knott. If you met her in the street and failed to acknowledge her, she would say 'Where is your bow?' Near the top of Orchard Hill is the Vicarage and here lived my favourite Vicar, not everybody's cup of tea, but a very polished gentleman. He was such a good talker and owned a sandy-coloured terrier, which would accompany him to Sunday School where he officiated.

At the Wheelwright Arms lived Mr Jack Smith, landlord and coal merchant who owned a white terrier who would lay in wait for the Vicar's dog, and then a proper shindy would commence. I well remember Mr Ford of Church Cottages trying to separate them with water, then pepper, if the Parson with his walking stick failed.

Children playing on Combe Road in Combe Down , 1910

Monkton Combe canal bridge

Ramble Seven ~
...Along the canal from Tucking Mill to Monkton Combe

The official public footpath now runs, from Midford, along the south bank of Midford Brook. Take the B3110 towards Hinton Charterhouse from Midford, and just after the bridge take the minor road to Limpley Stoke and the start of the footpath to Monkton Combe.

What is left to explore? Why, the Midford Brook and its environs. Why not the dried-up canal? Why had mankind discarded it? Much better to have left the water in especially as I was destined to set fire to it.

Below Tucking Mill canal bridge, toward the railway, the fallen beech leaves had collected, together with the dead outer leaves of reeds that grew there. It had been a very hot summer and everything was parched. As usual, with nothing much to do and with a box of matches in my pocket, it was only natural I should light a fire. It was only a small affair; usually you had to blow and strike a lot of matches, but today it was so easy. The gentle breeze through the valley fanned the flames and very soon it was out of control, and I knew the fate that awaited me if I was caught, so I scampered to the woods. Father was alerted at the Works by the smoke, and he and his mates had a rare old time beating it out with long nut sticks. My father was always ready to hand out punishment for misdemeanours and sometimes took off his belt to administer it. I often wondered why his trousers did not fall down.

Quite early in life I found out about father's liking for beer - instead of evaluating things in currency, he would say pints or ounces. If he did anything for somebody it was paid for in pints. After a day's work father would spruce up and go off the the Wheelwright's Arms. This was the moment I would wait for, and then I knew it was safe to go home for some tea. I would say that my father would never wallop you when you were asleep, so I was safe to the morning, and next day I might get away with just a clip around the ear hole.

First, we will go east toward the rising sun - the sun is always a feature in man's existence. We kids did not know much about it, just accepted the fact that it popped up over Kennel Farm in the morning, and was lost again over Midford Castle at night. The fact that it moves backward and forward along the hillside, describing an arc across the valley of Tucking Mill that waxed and waned with the seasons, did not concern us. Neither did the mystery of the changing colours of the countryside, the vagaries of the weather, the dawn chorus and the return of the nightingale, cuckoo, blackcap, chiffchaff and swallow in spring. The hot days of summer and the countless number of creatures and flowers, all contributed to the magic of Tucking Mill.

The logical place to start is in the Ponies Field. You reach this by taking the path to the cottages, passing along the rear of them where hops grow on the retaining bank of the canal, until we reach a gate near the toilet block. Here is the entrance to the Ponies Field. Mr Jack Harris, decorator of Monkton Combe, had a piebald pony that used to pull a cart containing his master's stock in trade. Mr Harris rented the Ponies Field from Mr Freeman of the Rag Mill, and was owner also of the cottages. The piebald pony was brought to graze, hence the 'Ponies Field'. What could it have been called before then? The valley of Tucking Mill was different before the coming of the canal.

If we take the towpath toward Monkton Combe, we are immediately faced with a fence across the way which we have to climb over. I remember just in front of the wire, we used to dig a sizable hole in the path, cover it in twigs and grass, hoping someone would put their foot in it. One day a gentleman obliged and got his foot wet as I had placed a saucepan of water at the bottom, of course he uttered dreadful threats at what he would do if he could catch us. We certainly did not give him the chance to to carry them out. Past the fence, the path very soon curves away to the left, and on the bend overlooking the Ponies Field, is a nice crab apple tree, and it is there today still providing some splendid fruit.

So here we are by the brook at the end of the hedge that separates the field from the cottager's gardens, here I remember a moorhen's nest. It was resting on two crossing willow branches in the centre of the brook - it contained just two eggs. A small group of us were crouched on the bank thinking of ways of obtaining those eggs without going into the water. I know, I said brightly, we will obtain two long nut sticks, we will attach a spoon on the end of one and a tin with some grass in on the other. We got the necessary apparatus and tried, one pair of hands controlling the spoon and another on the tin. The result was that both eggs finished up at the bottom of the brook. Oh well, we tried.

In the reeds of the canal, just opposite, I once found a moorhen's nest with eleven eggs; these were good food and I took the lot home, but it would have been better if I had found the nest earlier, for when mother cooked them for breakfast, some had to be discarded for they were nearly chickens.

Across from here is a piece of land trapped between the brook and the railway with no access unless you make use of a tortuous path used by anglers coming from Midford. Of course there was a bridge just about here, a few yards from the hedge, it was never attempted until Mr New, years later, took over the Ponies Field and the pasture known as Wilson's Field. Mr New very soon had a bridge, by the simple expedient of felling a tree across the stream and fitting a hand rail. Farmer Wilson, one time owner of Kennel Farm, must have retained what must have been a section of his land before the railway went through and so it was called Wilson's Field.

The farmer had a piece of cultivated land in the centre of his field where he used to spend some of his time growing potatoes; at the end of the summer he had to harvest the crop and get them over the brook - a fairly daunting task for one so old. Therefore, he appealed to Austin and me to dig them up and haul them along to the wire, up the railway embankment, across the bridge, and down the other side and along the Ponies Field, and store them in the annex to the toilet. It was a daunting task but we accomplished it carrying a few at a time. Farmer Wilson seemed pleased and rewarded us with one half-crown a piece.

At the same time he asked me to put the spade round the plot to make it look neat, which I agreed to do, not thinking that I would get paid for it. Imagine my surprise when he came again and forked out another half-crown - I felt quite guilty for I had not made much of a job of it - thinking it was an unpaid extra.

A year or two before this, my father and Mr Morris got the job of scything Wilson's Field, and Bill Morris and I were sent to the Wheelwright's Arms for a supply of beer which always seemed to be inseparable from haymaking. When we returned with the beverage, my father gave me a penny for going and Mr Morris, just being a bit posher said ' Bill shall I make up your savings to eighteen pence, will that be alright?' William said it was. It still puzzles me how they got that hay across the brook.

Following the course of the stream through the Ponies Field, we find that nearly all the trees on its banks are alders. Now, father was a bit of a medicine man and would harvest the cone-like berries, boil them in lovely spring water, drain off the grimy-looking liquid and bottle it. This elixir was guaranteed to cure boils and sold at a tanner a bottle. Whether it cured anybody, I don't know.

Just before we reach the small stream from the canal, I remember an episode that I still wonder about. I was going with a few friends on one of our usual adventures along the brookside, our purpose as usual was bird's nesting, especially moorhens. If we were successful the eggs would go into a tin of water and we would make a small fire and cook them to sustain us on our journey. The fascinating part of following the stream was that you would go on and on, always hoping to find treasure round the next bend, then suddenly you would realise that you were miles from home and must turn back. On this particular morning, there was a tall gentleman with a fishing rod on what we reckoned to be our territory, and we didn't like it. He said 'Hallo, lads, where are you going so bright and early?' I said we were going for a walk, at which he replied ' What, with a tin on a wire?' Then I knew he must be a detective sent down from Scotland Yard to catch boys with tins intent on robbing bird's nests which was against the law. I was so convinced at this that I ran back home leaving my companions nonplussed by the water.

The railway line of the Great Western was also the boundary between two worlds. The Tucking Mill side was sort of cosy and protected, but on the other it was wild and dangerous. Of course, everything belonged to Mr Hamlen; in actual fact it was rented. Then the woodland on the other side of the railway must be named 'Hamlen's Wood' and the big field on the south-side, 'Hamlen's Field'. That is the one you are confronted with across the brook south-east of the bridge. You clambered through a stile and went upward on a rough track. Here were riches indeed in summer: bird's nests, primroses, bluebells and wild asparagus among the wood. On the side near Hamlen's Field, was a walnut tree and a crab apple that had to be visited when we went along that way.

Hamlen's Field where the hayricks were built, was a copse in which there was always a magpie's nest, a wonderful affair in the top of a maple tree. We used to climb up and look at the marvel of nest building; it was a great ball of sticks with an alley way leading to the nest proper of grass and twigs. In a neighbouring tree was a jay's nest, a poor affair of mainly tree roots. This area reaching away towards Midford, was just a jumble of blackberry bushes where a few pounds could be collected in late summer.

The other side of Hamlen's Wood joined up with a section that belonged to Kennel Farm. Here was a great mass of hazel trees. In autumn, by shaking their narrow trunks, a hail of slip shells would descend on you, then with a small sack you could collect several pounds to take home to sell or eat at your leisure. I well remember being requested by the Vicar to blow the organ in the church, Mrs Picairn was the organist. My job was to pump a handle up and down watching an indicator to make sure there was enough wind to play the notes. When it was time for the sermon, and the Reverend climbed into the pulpit, I remained behind the scenes indulging in a repast of a few nuts. As I cracked them with my teeth, the acoustic of the church seemed to amplify the sound out of all reason. I persisted and the Reverend said afterwards 'How many nuts did you crack during the sermon, Stanley?' I said six, and he was glad I had told the truth for he must have counted them.

In the lower part of the farm section of the wood grew a hawthorn tree; it had struggled for years to get its head in the sunlight, consequently its branches which were not so lucky had died. At the top was a pigeon's nest and Austin decided to climb up and investigate. Reaching the top with a shower of twigs marking his progress, he shouted down, 'There are no eggs but two young birds', with that he grabbed one of them and the other fluttered down to be grabbed by me. Austin's effort had put undue strain on the branch he was standing on, and it gave way and he came crashing down through the old man's beard and blackberry vines, still holding the fledgling. He had only fallen about twelve feet and wasn't hurt and soon got over the shock. We set off home with the pigeons, intending to keep them for pets. I put my pigeon in the empty hen house but it died during the night. Next day Austin told me that his was also dead. When his father had seen it he said 'It won't live' and promptly wrung its neck for the pot.

Another attraction over the railway line was Kennel Farm itself. Austin was pally with the son, William, so this gave us a valid excuse to explore the whole of the farm area, which we were not slow at doing, not forgetting the extensive orchards behind and in front of Waterhouse.

I well remember the party given at the farm on the occasion of Bill's birthday. I was invited and went alone with Austin bearing four pence as a suitable birthday present. It was a funny party in as much as the grown-ups dined either before us in the same room or in some other part of the house. I remember rather a long table with plates of sandwiches, and more important, several flat apple tarts on big enamel plates.

I was fond of apple tart and must have eaten far more than four pence would have bought. Afterwards there were games in the big barn like rolling in the hay. I remember poor Jack, the hired help from a home, being buried in the hayrick and nearly suffocated. It wasn't much fun, but worth going for the apple tart.

To return to the Midford Brook where it passes under the railway, by climbing to the embankment and going down the other side without crossing the bridge, you can reach the Half-mile Meadow. I have never measured its length but it might be about that. The bottom of the bank is a stream that comes from a clay pipe in the retaining wall and runs into the brook. We did not pick the watercress that grew there for it was rumoured that it was part of the drainage system of the Vicarage. It was an awful long way from it but we did see an occasional soap sud moving down the surface of the water.

It was hereabouts, that Harold and I decided to build a shack and live free in the great outdoors. We had read in the Boys Own Paper how the cowboys on trail used to dig a hole for their hip and sleep under the stars - if they could do it, so could we. We obtained some corner posts from the Brake, nobody ever questioned that we could not, and these we embedded in the ground against the supporting wall of the railway. Cross pieces were fixed, nailed or tied with string, and twigs and grass piled on top on the roof. Whether it would keep out the rain was doubtful; it was never put to the test. Brother Philip decided to come as well and with a blanket each we settled down on the ground in our shack for the night.

As the gloom of the evening and the mist from the brook settled over the valley, it began to get cold, and we realised we were in for a long unpleasant night. Suddenly, I had a bright idea. Why not move over the railway into Arthur Gerrish's shack in the Ponies Field, which was far more professional and comfortable? With renewed enthusiasm we did this and settled down once more in our new accommodation. Very soon the cold and darkness weakened our resolve, and what a relief it was to hear mother's voice at the door of the shack - it was also a face saver for us stalwarts. After all if your mother was worrying that you might fall in the brook during the night, why, you had to allay her fears and go along home with her when she invited you to do so. Harold came as well and we all tumbled into the same bed and slept like heroes.

Although we were now convinced that camping out could be slightly overrated, Harold and I, next day returned to our very own shack in the Half-mile Meadow. We were a bit concerned to find the roof pushed in and then realised that the railway men had been burning the banks and it was the best thing to do to stop it catching fire. We set it to rights and decided to camp out all day and cook our own midday meal, which was always called 'dinner' by the poor.

We had a few things from home and decided to augment this with a few of Mr Styles's potatoes. Mr Styles had a piece of allotment by the side of the railway. We knew he was employed at the tramway depot at Bath, so would not be around to protest. So removing the soil from around the plants we took out the tubers, then carefully replaced the dirt and smoothed it over to conceal the fact that it had ever been disturbed. In a big jam tin, got from the rubbish heap, half-filled with water, I cooked the spuds over a small fire. At one o'clock, they were cooked and I shared them them out on a couple of enamel plates. I remember Harold saying 'Give me some of the gravy, I likes that'. I gave him a plateful - it was only salt water, but it is amazing the likes and dislikes of juveniles.

Here the end of the existing Coal Canal is in sight. On the right, now, is a place of elders and blackthorn, from which we used to taste the sloes and announce that they were as sour as always. A ditch across the path drains the water from the old canal into the brook. There is a fence made of timber to shut in the pasture land, and a wire fence to guard the railway. Although the railway property was private, the general public would venture on it on a Sunday when there were no trains. This was a favourite walk for the family, when father decided to take us. On the way, he would show us how to fashion a posy of wild flowers. He usually started it by the canal with the largest thistle head he could find for the centre, around it he would put moon daisies, hardheads, teasels, red clover, snapdragons, ragged robins, cuckoo flowers and even yarrow.

From the canal we climbed through the wire on to the railway. We could follow the railway past Chancys Rocks, select the best blooms that grew in profusion on the banks, until we reached the crossing gates near Mill Lane Railway Station or if you are a film fan, 'Titfield', where some of the film was made of *The Titfield Thunderbolt*.

From here we took the road to the Freeman's Rag Mill, which wound its way past the mill and along the side of the College playing fields, known to us as the 'Cricket Field' and no other. Of course, father's ultimate destination was the pub or the Viaduct Inn, which you reach by climbing a slope just beyond the Eleven Arches. By now the posy was complete and we were allowed to take it home after being refreshed by ginger beer and biscuits on the lawn. Father remained to closing time.

However, let us get on in exploring Midford Brook. The meadow is very low-lying and often flooded, so it is a place of small pools of mud and water; it fills up the gap between the brook and the retaining wall of the railway. Just beyond a drain that crosses our path to the brook, is a weir. Here the brook divides, the upper artificial section provides a head of water to drive the waterwheel at Freeman's Mill, now known as Kritch Kraft. The water allowed to go over the weir is taken away by the lower brook that passes under the footpath that takes you to Waterhouse and up Stout Hill. On the way it receives the water from the mill after it has done its work driving the waterwheel, in so doing, it formed an area of land known as Freeman's Meadow, into an island.

Before the brook reaches the College playing fields, it circulates round a small island in its centre and island of rabbits. So on to the Cricket Ground as it was known; here I once played cricket for the village against the College boys. I was not much of a cricket player at the age of twelve and only got in the team because one of their star performers was at the Viaduct, too inebriated to play. We batted first and did not do very well; if I had made a century, we must have won, but I remember hitting the first ball bowled at me with all my might, and the College boys cried 'Jolly good hit, it must be a six'. A six was put on the score sheet and I got ready for the next ball. I missed it altogether and it took the middle stump out of the ground. I must have been in at least two minutes and was credited with the second highest score. We must have lost, the top batsman only made seventeen.

From the Cricket Ground, the brook passes under the Eleven Arches and the Warminster Road and joins the River Avon.

There are various alternative ways in getting back to the bridge at Tucking Mill, but we will return in thought only. As Bernard Shaw once said 'If you want to travel to the stars you must do so in thought only'.

Stanley Wicks
1910 ~ 1996

Acknowledgments

The Combe Down Heritage Society would like to thank Carlene Fuller and Pauline Upward for their help in finding photographs of Stanley Wicks; John Brooke for information on Southstoke; Kit Powell for checking some walks; Jane Briggs for her local knowledge; Malcolm Aylett for some recent photographs; Lisa Pentreath for designing this book, and Toby Pentreath and Ben Smith for posing as boys of the 1920's on the cover.

COMBE DOWN HERITAGE SOCIETY
a sustainable future for heritage

This publication was made possible by a grant from Awards For All. The Combe Down Heritage Society is supported by Bath and North East Somerset Council, Hydrock and Wessex Water.